THE OFFICIAL

DOWNTON ABBEY CHRISTMAS COOKBOOK

THE OFFICIAL

DOWNTON ABBEY CHRISTMAS COOKBOOK

REGULA YSEWIJN

weldon**owen**

CONTENTS

FOREWORD

One of my abiding childhood memories was the digging up and bringing in of the Christmas tree (this was in the days before the roots were habitually cut off). It would later be replanted in a grove of past holiday trees at the end of the kitchen garden. Of course, in those days, Christmas did not begin until December—late in December—but when it did, it was the most wonderful time of the year.

We made five Christmas specials for *Downton Abbey*, each a feature-length episode with its own story arc. They all contained crucial plot points for the overall story but also allowed us to meet new, sometimes one-off characters and experience the wider world of Downton. Some will remember them best for such momentous events as Matthew's snowbound proposal to Mary; the birth of Matthew and Mary's son, George; or Matthew's death. Others will remember the release of Anna from prison and her reunion with Bates; the birth of Edith's daughter, Marigold; or the departure of Tom and Sybbie for America. But around these deeply moving scenes we also see the future Edward VIII saved from scandal, we shoot grouse in the Highlands, and we dance with the bright, young things in the beautifully lit ballrooms of the London season.

Christmas would be nothing without its food, of course, and indeed its drink. Flemish food writer and culinary historian Regula Ysewijn has brought to life not only the dishes of the Downton era but also some of the magnificent edible delights of earlier centuries. It is a brilliantly researched book full of tasty treats. I do hope you enjoy it.

Julian Fellowes
London, 2020

A DELICIOUSLY DIFFERENT CHRISTMAS

Christmas may be a wonderful time of the year, but it's also one of the most nostalgic. It's easy to believe that Christmas has never changed—that we've always eaten turkey and roast potatoes, Brussels sprouts and plum pudding, mince pies and Christmas cake. But I suspect that if you aren't British, you will be frowning even reading these words.

Every country, every family has its own way of celebrating Christmas. One family's sacrosanct tradition is another's worst nightmare. The British love of dark, fruity flavors goes back to the medieval period, but even in Britain, more and more people are turning to cheesecake or chocolate to end their yuletide feast. Traditions change, and it turns out that even Christmas hasn't always been the same.

In *The Official Downton Abbey Cookbook*, I showcased some of the popular dishes from 1912 to 1930. Those who are familiar with the book will know that the food of the era can be very different from that of today, but that ultimately, good recipes stand the test of time.

This is a beautiful book that goes beyond the expected foods of Christmas to show us delights we've long forgotten. Regula's customary combination of solid research and gastronomic flair has unearthed a world of often surprising recipes seen through the lens of *Downton Abbey*. You'll discover such delights as the Whitby cake, which the Dowager Countess would have remembered but which would have been virtually unknown to her granddaughters, and the delicious hackin pudding, a holiday tradition of northern England.

For me, Christmas wouldn't be Christmas without a Boxing Day breakfast of fried plum pudding and bacon. For the Crawleys and their staff, it would be nothing without a bowl of steaming punch. As for you, I'm sure this book will give you something deliciously Downton to add to your own traditions.

Annie Gray
London, 2020

INTRODUCTION

At Downton Abbey, Christmas 1919 begins in the early-morning hours with a commotion deep in the woods ending the night silence. A large, dew-shrouded fir is cut from its roots, bound onto the back of a lorry, and then transported quickly along a tire-rutted, tree-lined path. Before any family members are awake, Thomas coordinates the tree's swift unloading for setup in the great hall. Meanwhile, the fires are lit across the house, maids on their knees, their hands covered in soot from the coals. Light floods into the rooms as heavy, dark drapes are drawn one after the other. Downstairs, Mrs. Patmore and Daisy have already finished the food for the family's breakfast, and Daisy has gone upstairs for her other duties.

On her way down, Daisy passes the great hall, her arms heavily laden with cleaner and a bucket of coals. She is stopped in her steps by the sheer brilliance of the grand tree and takes in the spectacle, amazed. Whereas before the tree was bare, it is now shimmering with silver tinsel and sparkling garlands. Edith, watched by her sister Mary, is hanging a lovely ornament on a branch, while Lord Grantham and Carson are deep in conversation and gesturing toward the fir. Mrs. Hughes, who has just criticized Daisy for dawdling and sent her off downstairs, is now taking in the majestic tree herself, right in time for the illumination of the new electric lights strung among its branches. Not surprisingly, such bright lights are not welcomed by everyone. The candles

of the past, which cast the tree in a more delicate light, are still favored by the Dowager Countess. It is tradition, she would say, and tradition is what Christmas is all about.

Some may mistakenly believe that the Christmas feast we see served later in the day at Downton is centuries old, but it is actually rooted in Victorian times. Many of the customs associated with Christmas are much older, however, going back to a time when winter was all about surviving the darkest, dreariest, coldest, and most dangerous time of the year.

In ancient Rome, the multiple-day festival of Saturnalia, held in honor of the agricultural god Saturn, was celebrated from December 17 through December 23. People decorated their houses with greenery, sat down to huge feasts, exchanged gifts, and lit candles. Role reversal was popular too, with masters dressing like servants and men like women. This was a phenomenon in Britain in medieval times as well, when men of the lower classes could be lords for the day and the little boys could be bishops. An echo of these practices is played out in season 2, episode 9, when we see the servants wearing paper crowns at Christmas lunch.

Beginning in the late third century, Saturnalia was immediately followed on December 25 by the feast of Sol Invictus (the Unconquered Sun), which marked the gradual return to longer days after the winter solstice, the darkest day of the year. In the Northern Hemisphere, the latter can fall on any day from December 20 through December 23. Early in the fourth century, under the reign of Emperor Constantine, Christianity became the dominant religion of the Roman Empire, and in the year 336, Christmas was formally celebrated on December 25 for the first time, a date some scholars believe was chosen in order to diminish the popular pagan celebrations that filled those calendar weeks. Christmas would not become a major holiday of Christianity for another six centuries, however.

Mumming, which has its origins in Saturnalia and goes back a millennium in Britain, was a popular practice for everything from Samhain, the early Gaelic festival that became All Hallows Eve and All Saints' Day, to a thirteenth-century Christmastime wedding at the court of Edward I. During the Christmas season, it called for dressing up in elaborate costumes—so elaborate the mummers would not be recognizable to those who knew them—and going door-to-door in the neighborhood or in a nearby village. If the mummers—also known as "guisers"—were welcomed into a home, they would typically perform a dance or song or skit to the delight of their audience, who would then try to identify their cleverly disguised visitors and offer them food and drink. This custom had a dark side as well, with wandering bands of drunken, masked mummers reportedly engaging in inappropriate behavior, which prompted the banning of mummery by Henry VIII for a period.

By the eighteenth century, mummers were formalized in traveling theater troupes that performed plays everywhere from village squares to concert halls. Today, the village of Bampton in the Cotswolds, which was used for a number of outdoor scenes in *Downton Abbey*—the library stood in for the entrance to the Cottage Hospital and

the vicarage for the exterior of Isobel Crawley's house—has a resident mummers troupe that performs each year on Christmas Eve.

Early Nordic and Germanic peoples had their own winter solstice festival called Yule (or Yuletide, for Yule time). A central part of the celebration, which drew on an earlier tradition of bonfires, was the Yule log (it was an actual log and not the buttercream cake made to look like one we know today), which was dragged from the forest, carved with wishes and spells, ignited with a piece of the Yule log saved from the previous year, and then left to burn for twelve days to ensure good luck and prosperity in the coming year. By the seventeenth century, the tradition had migrated to England, as illustrated by this excerpt from "Come Bring the Noise," a carol by English poet Robert Herrick (1591–1674):

> *Come bring the noise,*
> *My merry, merry boys,*
> *The Christmas log to the firing;*
> *While my good dame, she*
> *Bids ye all be free,*
> *And drink to your heart's desiring.*
>
> *With the last year's brand*
> *Light the new block, and*
> *For good success in his spending,*
> *On your psaltries play,*
> *That sweet luck may*
> *Come while the log is a teending.*

This tradition of which Herrick writes was still widely practiced, albeit on a smaller scale, in Edwardian England and is visible at Downton, where a Yule log crackles in the fire not far from the family's grandly decorated holiday tree.

A SEASON OF FEASTING AND FRIVOLTY

In medieval Catholic Britain, over half of the days of the year were fast days, with all animal products—meat, eggs, dairy—prohibited. By the seventeenth century, the restrictions had been reduced to the forty days of Lent, Fridays, and many holy days. Anyone discovered defying the rule was subject to a fine, which the rich gladly paid. Fish was allowed, however, and its definition was surprisingly broad. It included beaver tail, barnacle geese, and seals—in other words, if it lived in or near the water, it was fish and therefore permitted. But despite the importance of Christmas on the religious calendar, meat was allowed on the holiday table, and so Christmas turned into the meat-focused feast still enjoyed today. Indeed, Christmas appeared to be more about feasting than it was about the birth of Christ.

The Christmas season beginning in December 1065 was an eventful one, with the death of King Edward (Edward the Confessor) on January 4 and the crowning of Harold II on January 6. Harold was the first monarch to be crowned in Westminster Abbey, which had been consecrated on December 28, little more than a week earlier. By Christmas 1066, Harold was himself dead, with William I (William the Conqueror) crowned the new king on December 25. The following year, William reportedly hosted a grand Christmas feast in London to gain the favor of his subjects.

Some 350 years later, Richard II, who had recently reopened the Parliament's massive Westminster Hall (which had been built under William II in 1097) after ordering an expansion and various embellishments to the original structure, hosted a Christmas feast in the hall that boasted "twenty-eight oxen and three hundred sheep, and game and fowls without number, feeding ten thousand guests for many days." The occasion was accompanied by pageants and plays and other entertainments typical of the time.

During the Christmas season of 1399, the Earls of Huntington, Kent, and Salisbury, among others, plotted to gain access to Windsor Castle under the pretense of holiday guising, where they hoped to capture Henry IV and restore the deposed Richard II to the throne. Their planned rebellion, which became known as the Epiphany Rising, was thwarted by one of their own betraying them to the king, however, who promptly left London. The conspirators, who fled to the countryside, all met a violent end. The imprisoned Richard also never saw another Christmas, though exactly how he met his demise is unknown.

Encouraged by Henry VII, Italian historian Polydore Vergil, who spent most of his life in England, wrote *Anglia Historia,* a history of England, which he finished in 1513 but would not be published for another two decades. In it he notes that it was the custom of the English as early as the reign of Henry II (1133 to 1189) to celebrate Christmas with "plays, masques, and magnificent spectacles, together with games as dice and dancing, which . . . were not customary with other nations." Vergil also mentions the appointment of a Lord of Misrule, who was chosen to oversee the entertainments, which, in addition to organized events, typically included wild partying and excessive amounts of drink.

BATES
Ssh. We'll worry about everything else later, but for now, let's just have a very happy Christmas.

~ SEASON 5, EPISODE 9

In the Tudor era, specifically during the reign of Henry VII, who adored Christmas, the festival became an even more lavish and rowdy affair, with pageants and plays, games—backgammon, chess, cards—and religious services, feasting and imbibing. During the Christmas season of 1512, on Epiphany, Henry VIII hosted a masked ball inspired by Italy—"a thing not seen afore in England." Opulent displays, extravagant processions, lively holiday pantomimes played by courtiers, and even mock hunting scenes became part of the annual spectacle. One year, according to *English Forests and Forest Trees*, published in 1853, "an artificial forest was drawn in by a lion and an antelope, the hides of which were richly embroidered with golden ornaments; the animals were harnessed with chains of gold, and on each sat a fair damsel in gay apparel." The royal feasting table included the grandest of dishes, with swans, peacocks, incredibly large and richly decorated mince pies, and even larger fruitcakes. But the most important dish at the Christmas feast was the boar's head, which had been secured by a royal hunting party and was ceremoniously paraded into the imposing dining hall.

The nobility of the period started to imitate the Christmas splendor of the court—both the feasting and the pageantry—at their own stately homes and at the Inns of Court. The working classes were allowed greater privileges at Christmas, too. In 1494, during the reign of Henry VII, an act that specifically forbade beggars and vagabonds from engaging in unlawful games to win the wages of workers also forbade

"Artificiers, Labourers, Servants, or Apprentices, to play at any games, except at Christmas." In fact, recreation was encouraged at Christmas, but there were exceptions. For example, the lower classes still held on to the pagan tradition of mumming, though the authorities tried to prohibit it, as they believed it too often led to rioting and even murder. Some mummers were not even disguised, as they could not afford masks, instead just darkening their faces with soot.

The Twelve Days of Christmas, or Christmastide, which extended from December 25 to January 5, the eve of Epiphany, were a time of general merrymaking, of song and dance, of food and frivolity, of visiting neighbors and friends. December 25 was all about the feast—both the food and the splendor—with little thought given to Christ's birth. On December 26, the feast day of Saint Stephen, the first Christian martyr, the nobility typically gave their household servants, who had spent Christmas Day serving them, the day off to see their families, sending them out with small gifts and sometimes leftover food from the holiday table. A lord would also give a gift to his tenant farmer, and the farmer would reciprocate with perhaps a couple of hens, an exchange that would have been stipulated in their contract. In other words, it was a business transaction. For the poorest people, donations were made to alms boxes in churches, the contents of which were distributed on December 26. This custom of the rich giving to the poor on Saint Stephen Day was the precursor to Boxing Day (see page 90), which became a public holiday in 1871.

At court, Henry VIII distributed gifts on New Year's but also received gifts from all his courtiers. One year, Anne Boleyn gave the king a set of spears used for one of his favorite holiday pastimes, wild boar hunting. It was a capital move from Anne, as he married her about a year later.

Mary I, the daughter of Henry VIII, made an unsuccessful attempt to reverse the Protestant reforms of her father, hoping to make England a Catholic nation once more. During her reign, she did reduce the extravagance of the Christmas celebrations, but on her death, the elaborate holiday festivities of her father were promptly revived when Elizabeth I, her half sister, was crowned in 1559.

Elizabeth was set to enjoy her life and loved music, dancing, and theater, especially the plays of William Shakespeare. She spent a tremendous amount of money on every feast, as she liked to display her wealth with opulence. These lines from "Christmas Husbandry Fare," a poem of the era by Thomas Tusser (1515–80), describes the festive food of the time, with turkey making an early appearance:

> They both do provide against Christmas
>   do come,
> To welcome their neighbour, good cheer to
>   have some;
> Good bread and good drink, a good fire in
>   the hall,
> Brawn pudding and souse, and good
>   mustard withal.

> Beef, mutton, and pork, shred pies of the best,
> Pig, veal, goose, and capon, and turkey well
>   dressed;
> Cheese, apples, and nuts, jolly carols to hear,
> As then in the country is counted good cheer.

Some of the foods associated with Christmas, such as mince pies and spiced fruitcakes and buns, were eaten on special occasions year-round. But that ended in 1592, when the London office that oversaw markets issued a decree halting the sale of spiced baked goods except for funerals,

Christmas, or Good Friday, firmly linking these prized sweets to religious events.

The Reformation lead to the rise of Puritanism, and in the seventeenth century, the increasing dislike for any Catholic customs. Puritans claimed Charles I, who had married the Catholic daughter of Henry IV of France, had too much affinity with her faith and feared he would weaken the official establishment of the reformed Church of England. In 1644, an act of Parliament banned the celebration of Christmas. It stipulated that the feast should be abolished, and that the sins of our forefathers should be remembered for they "turned this Feast, pretending the Memory of Christ, into an extreme Forgetfulness of him, by giving Liberty to carnal and sensual Delights, being contrary to the Life which Christ led here on Earth. . . ." In other words, the celebrants were having way too much fun on Christmas. Three years later, in 1647, an ordinance was passed that reiterated the abolishment of the feast.

England became a republic under Oliver Cromwell, who ruled England, Scotland, and Ireland from 1653 until his death just five years later. Cromwell made his dislike for any form of feasting clear, discarding it as mere popery. If only Henry VIII could have known that his ending of the authority of the Roman Catholic Church over the Church of England would lead to the abolishment of his favorite festival. But this does not mean that people didn't continue to celebrate Christmas in secret: During Christmas 1652, the great memoirist John Evelyn mentions in his diary, rather disgruntledly, "Christmas day, no sermon anywhere, no church being permitted to be open, so observed it at home." Three years later, he remarks that no notice of Christmas Day was taken, but in 1657, he goes to hear a secret sermon in London's Exeter Chapel, which is soon surrounded by soldiers. Evelyn is questioned as to "why, contrary to

the ordinance made that none should any longer observe the superstitious times of the Nativity," he is praying on Christmas. He is dismayed to be disturbed in trying to pray for Christ and for Charles II, who is in exile, but he accepts that he got off fairly easily given that the soldiers threatened all the worshippers with muskets.

The year 1660 marked both the return of Charles II to the throne and the first legal celebration of Christmas since 1644. Charles was nicknamed The Merry Monarch because he used any excuse to throw a big, extravagant party. Outside of the court, Christmas was making a comeback more slowly, as is evident in the rather modest festivities described by England's favorite seventeenth-century diarist, Samuel Pepys. On December 24, he mentions making the house ready "to-morrow being Christmas day." On December 25, he goes to church in the morning, then has dinner (at that time, a midday meal) with his wife and his brother, feasting on mutton and a chicken. After dinner, he goes to church again, and that's about it for Christmas cheer. The custom of the Christmas box, which has its roots in the alms boxes of the Middle Ages, also returns with the monarchy. On December 19, 1663, Pepys describes going to pay his shoemaker and giving "something to the boys' box against Christmas."

Recipe collections of the period do not mention Christmas, though mince pies, fruitcakes, and plum pudding do appear in them in great numbers. By the eighteenth century, the endless feasting associated with the Twelve Days of Christmas had begun to disappear. Henry Bourne's *Antiquitates Vulgares: Or the Antiquities of the Common People*, published in 1725, chronicled the old traditions of Christmas and had little positive to say about them. Bourne compared the custom of caroling to rioting and deemed mumming and gift giving on New Year's superstitious and sinful.

More and more people were working in factories and did not want to lose twelve days of pay, as it would mean they may not be able to afford food or their rent. But the upper classes also no longer participated in the excessive, multiday feasting common in the past, deeming it wild and improper. The Christmas food tradition was moving to the privacy of the home, where it was a relatively quiet family celebration rather than a rowdy public one.

In his comprehensive late eighteenth-century book, *Observations on Popular Antiquities*, John Brand writes of how a 1708 issue of the magazine *London Bewitched* reported favorably on the popularity of the season and of the ingredient still associated with Christmas today: "Grocers will now begin to advance their plumbs, and bellmen will be very studious concerning their Christmas verses." Plumbs, or raisins, are the main ingredient of Christmas fruitcake and Christmas plum pudding, the latter among the most adored and most patriotic dishes of the century, served with roast beef, another element of national pride. The magazine then goes on to report on the opposing Puritan side, though the editors clearly don't agree with it: "Fanaticks will begin to preach down superstitious *minc'd pyes* and abominable plumb porridge; and the Church of England will highly stand up for the old Christmas hospitality."

HOLIDAY TRADITIONS, OLD AND NEW

In the nineteenth century, the British began looking to the past for lost Christmas traditions that could be revived in the present. This nostalgia for the old ways produced many of the Christmas customs seen in the Downton era and still practiced today. Christmas carols, lost when the rule of Cromwell forbade them, were brought back to life, and new books of carols appeared. Thomas Hervey's *The Book of Christmas*, published in 1836 and illustrated by Robert Seymour, one of the most successful caricaturists of the era, gives a comprehensive account of English Christmas customs in the early nineteenth century. In it the reader sees illustrations of a Christmas still recognizable today, with holly sprig–decorated plum pudding together with roast beef at the center of the holiday table, mince pies, enormous racks of beef bought and sold in the streets, and a carriage full of turkeys.

Christmas literature as a new discipline became popular in the Victorian period, finding its roots in Shakespeare's seventeenth-century *The Winter's Tale* and in the early nineteenth-century ghost stories of Lord Byron, Mary Shelley, and John Polidori. Frightening people around Christmastime drew on the scary guises of mummers in the past. In 1835, Charles Dickens published "Christmas Festivities," his first essay about Christmas, in a London weekly newspaper. In it he explains how Christmas should be enjoyed as both a time of reflection and a family occasion: "A Christmas family party! We know nothing in nature more delightful!" In the same essay, he breathes new life into a forgotten custom that was, according to contemporary historian Mark Forsyth, popular in England between 1720 and 1784: kissing under the mistletoe. In those days, a berry had to be picked from the mistletoe sprig before each kiss.

By December 1843, when *A Christmas Carol* was published, the revival of Christmas was in full

MERTON

Well, if you're going to be miserable, you might as well do it in charming surroundings.

~ SEASON 5, EPISODE 9

swing. A few books detailing the celebration of Christmas, such as Hervey's *The Book of Christmas* and *The Keeping of Christmas at Bracebridge Hall* by Washington Irving (1820), had come earlier, but Dickens's book quickly proved the most popular. *A Christmas Carol* basically became the guidebook for a traditional English Christmas, as it had everything for a perfect holiday story: ghosts, an evil tightwad in remorse, hard times and hunger, charity, a feast with a large turkey, a decorated tree, and a happy ending.

Inspired in part by Dickens, who quickly turned out four more Christmas novels, Christmas soon became the highlight of the annual calendar, much in the same way centuries earlier it had been a way of coping with the darkest and coldest season of the year, especially for those living at the lower rungs of society. To help working people save up for this festive winter celebration, many grocery stores and pubs operated Christmas clubs, which enabled folks to put away a little money every week or so for holiday luxuries.

But the upper class embraced these revived traditions, too, sitting down to a Christmas feast and outfitting trees with candles and glittery decorations. The Christmas tree, which was documented in a more modest form in England as early as the fifteenth century, experienced renewed interest with the 1840 arrival in London of Albert, the German prince consort. From that year forward, Victoria and Albert included a beautifully decorated tree at Windsor as part of their holiday celebration, and as the monarchs were admired across English society, houses both grand and simple soon wanted a tree, too.

Nostalgia was selling well, so traders began offering Christmas-branded items, such as books and cards. Although the first Christmas card in England was reportedly sent to James I by a German physician in the early seventeenth century, Sir Henry Cole, a civil servant and art shop owner, is credited with commissioning and marketing the first commercial cards in 1843. Some cards showed happy families, but the two best sellers depicted a Christmas plum pudding in the middle of a festive table and a somewhat bizarre rendering of a plum pudding dressed up like a little man. What rarely appeared on the cards was any reference to the birth of Christ. The English Christmas favored the secular, and Father Christmas, who first appeared in the mid-seventeenth century, was the traditional personification of the season, having pushed the story of the nativity further into the background.

By the Edwardian era, Selfridges, Harrods, and other department stores were popularizing the custom of buying Christmas gifts. They created elaborate holiday window displays that were lit up at night to catch the eye of passersby. Christmas gift fairs and ingredients and guidelines for a perfect holiday meal were advertised in newspapers. And more than ever, Christmas revolved around the importance of family and not religion. In the *Downton Abbey* Christmas episode at the end of season 5, family togetherness is strong. Atticus feels properly part of the family for the first time, and family ties are making Tom doubt his move to Boston with his daughter, Sybbie. Marigold is accepted into the family as Edith's daughter by Robert, Mr. Bates and Anna are reunited, and even Violet and Isobel are having a moment over a cup of wassail.

In the spirit of the season, efforts were made to put aside all differences and to forget all worries to achieve the perfect Christmas. As Mr. Bates puts it perfectly, "We'll worry about everything else later. But for now, let's just have a very happy Christmas."

CHRISTMAS TRADITIONS

CHRISTMAS TREE

In his *Survey of London*, first published in 1598, John Stow writes of reading a 1444 account describing not only the decorating of the house and the church for Christmas but also of a tree: "... at the Leadenhall, in Cornhill, a Standard of tree, being set up in the midst of the pavement, fast in the ground, nailed full of holme and ivie, sor disport of Christmas to the people." Stow's research shows us that trees were part of the "evergreen decking," or decorations, used at the winter solstice as early as the fifteenth century and most likely even before that.

However, the tree would not become a symbol of Christmas until the Victorian period, aided by the royal public relations campaign it received when Victoria and Albert and their family were pictured around their decorated tree in an engraving in the *Illustrated London News* in 1848. In Germany, Albert's birthplace, the Christmas tree had long been popular, and Albert was a great champion of the custom in his new home. People were anxious to get themselves a tree to mimic what they saw the royals doing, just as many people today like to copy whatever celebrities are doing.

By 1850, the decorated Christmas tree was well established in England, and Charles Dickens wrote an extensive essay on the subject, in which he noted, "I have been looking on, this evening, at a merry company of children assembled round that pretty German toy, a Christmas Tree."

CHRISTMAS DECORATIONS

In *The Book of Days*, Robert Chambers, a prominent nineteenth-century Scottish author, publisher, and evolutionary thinker, writes that the custom of decorating with real flowers and greenery is "instinctive in human nature; and we accordingly find scarcely any nation, civilised or savage, with which it has not become more or less familiar." An evidence of this practice is the use of evergreens for "decking" not only the home and the church but also the streets during the Christmas season.

Greens you can use to create your own Downton-style Christmas decorations are holly, ivy, rosemary, laurel or bay, evergreen oak, yew, cypress, and box. (Interestingly, ivy would never be used in churches because of its association with Bacchus, the god of wine, and box, once used for decorating gingerbread, is poisonous when ingested.) Homemade paper chains and other decorations appeared in the Downton era and can also be easily re-created today (see page 50).

In Edwardian England, according to popular custom, all of these Christmas decorations had to be taken down the evening of Twelfth Night, the day before Epiphany. But in the past, the greens would not have been removed until the evening of February 1, the day before Candlemas (the traditional end of the Christmas-Epiphany season), as these few lines from a Candlemas Eve carol by seventeenth-century poet Robert Herrick illustrate:

Down with the rosemary, and so
Down with the bays and mistletoe;
Down with the holly, ivy, all
Wherewith ye decks the Christmas hall; . . .

CHRISTMAS GIFTS

In 1847, Thomas "Tom" Smith, a London baker and confectioner who operated a shop on Goswell Road, patented the Christmas cracker. These still-popular holiday table decorations were initially simply pretty paper wrapped around candies. Later, Smith added a strip of paper printed with a lucky motto or a love message to each cracker, and later still, sweets-filled crackers coexisted alongside crackers containing inexpensive jewelry or other gifts. Smith did not add the "crack" to his invention until 1860, when a strip of saltpeter was slipped into each cracker. After Smith's death in 1869, his sons took over the business, and by the Downton era, paper hats and more elaborate gifts were being tucked into the crackers. In season 2, episode 9, the Downton staff is seen wearing crown-like hats from their Christmas crackers at their holiday lunch. (To make Christmas crackers for an authentic Downton period celebration, see page 207.)

Tom Smith and Company's advertisements at Christmastime always showed an iconic Father Christmas and outlined all the "Christmas novelties" on offer. There were fancy boxes, decorative wreaths, and French, English, and American confections, as well as "Santa Claus surprise stockings"—filled with toys and games—an idea imported from America.

Christmas grew in importance in the Victorian era, and gift giving, which had been traditional at New Year's, moved to Christmas. In the beginning, the gifts were modest—sweets or other foods, handmade trinkets—and were often hung on the tree. As the gifts grew in size and value, they moved under the tree.

In *Downton Abbey*, we witness gift giving in season 2. The year is 1919, and the staff is gathered around the Christmas tree. Each is given a useful item, such as fabric for a new frock, tied with a piece of string, for the women. Lady's maids and butlers would maybe receive a little extra, as we also see when Mr. Carson is given a book about the royal families of Europe and Lady Mary tops Anna's gift of cloth with a heart-shaped brooch. None of the gifts for the servants is wrapped, as festive wrapping paper was still a novelty, sold for the first time commercially in the United States, in Kansas, in 1919. It is possible that Cora's mother sent her daughter a few sheets, because when we see the family exchange gifts during their traditional Christmas lunch, we see boxes wrapped in colorful paper. Unlike the gifts the family gives to the staff, the ones they exchange among themselves were not meant to be useful. They were solely for pleasure.

By 1920, Christmas shopping was widely advertised, and towns were typically full of shoppers ahead of the holiday. Newspapers printed extra Christmas supplements full of advice and stories to get readers through the celebration. In that same year, the *Sheffield Independent* published *The Book of Christmas Cheer*, which included chapters on how to cook a turkey and make a plum pudding and on how to play all kinds of parlor games. Another chapter was devoted to Christmas presents and how to select the ideal gift for a friend. Consumerism was taking off, and Christmas became all about spending your hard-earned cash for the perfect Christmas.

By Christmas 1924, festive wrapping paper had become more common, even for the working class, and we see Mrs. Hughes hiding in her office wrapping gifts for Mr. Carson. She even uses brightly colored ribbons for the bows.

CHRISTMAS ENTERTAINMENT

In the past, Christmas entertainment was a decadent and often mischievous affair, but by the Edwardian period, such costly and boisterous practices were no longer popular and families were establishing new traditions. At Downton Abbey, playing charades was a Christmas Eve tradition. Other families might have preferred card games or performing a skit or play, or there could be music and singing. The New Year's hunt, a driven pheasant shoot (as birds are flushed into the sky, hunters rotate among ten stations, each with a different terrain), is another Downton tradition. Everyone would be clad in tweed, rifle under the arm, ready to practice this ancient aristocratic pastime reminiscent of the wild boar hunts of medieval days. The shoot would be followed by a luncheon at the shooting lodge, yet another longstanding tradition of the season.

CHRISTMAS CAROLS

In season 5, episode 9, we see the Crawley family and their staff gather together in the great hall before the Christmas tree to sing carols. The tradition of singing carols at home likely dates back only a century or so, but Christmas carols themselves—or at least hymns with Christian themes—are much older. Some of the earliest Christmas carols documented in England are found in a 1426 work by John Audelay, a priest and poet living in the western part of the country who recorded the words to twenty-five "caroles of Cristemas," most likely songs sung by local wassailers of the time.

Roughly a century later, in the Tudor period, caroling became popular, and even Henry VIII was known to have sung a carol or two. Most of the songs were religion based, though some were secular and spoke of hunting and feasting. For example, the then-popular "Boar's Head Carol" describes the tradition of hunting a wild boar and ceremonially parading its head at the Christmas feast. This is most certainly a carryover from the pagan and Nordic customs of sacrificing animals to implore the gods for a prosperous New Year, a practice Christians assimilated into their own celebrations. By 1521, *Christmasse Carolles*, one of the earliest printed collections of carols in England, was published in London by Jan van Wynkyn de Worde, a German immigrant.

With the arrival of Puritan rule in the mid-seventeenth century, Christmas festivities, including caroling, were banned as being impious. A century later, the Victorians set about reviving many old Christmas traditions, including the singing of medieval carols. In his 1833 *Christmas Carols, Ancient and Modern*, author William Sandys despairs that celebrating Christmas is "on the wane" and offers up some eighty carols, including some "specimen of French Provincial Carols," probably in an attempt to make the idea of caroling more attractive—and, given the French connection, even fashionable.

CORA

Please be careful on Christmas Eve if you do decide to drink. You'll get plastered on a sniff of sherry.

ROBERT

Paradise.

~ SEASON 5, EPISODE 9

KITCHEN NOTES

For this book, I've worked with original recipes in cookbooks from the nineteenth and early twentieth centuries, with one excursion into the earliest cookery book in the English language. Although Mrs. Patmore projects a humble background, she would have had to be esteemed to work in a large English country house like Downton Abbey, and given her age, her training would have come from the books of such nineteenth-century authors as Eliza Acton, Isabella Beeton, and Charles Francatelli, among others. Nearly all of the recipes in this book would have been familiar to her with the exception of some post–World War I discoveries, such as the spinach balls on page 144.

The recipes in the following pages will give you the opportunity to host a Downton-inspired Christmas with dishes that are still relevant today. Some of them have hardly changed over the last hundred years; others have evolved to suit the contemporary need for a lighter option. For example, vegetables are cooked for a shorter time, and béchamel is not used nearly as much as it was even twenty years ago. As a child of the 1980s, I recall that many of our family dinners came with a layer of white sauce, just as suppers did in the Downton era.

When it comes to a Downton-style Christmas, it is all about the main roast, the trimmings, and the puddings, and I've given options for each of these elements. There are festive fish dishes, impressive birds, flavorsome game, and emblematic beef. Christmas pudding, cake, and other celebratory sweets are plentiful, so take your pick and savor the seasonal flavors of warm spices, candied citrus peel, and dried fruits. And whether you are just back from a wintry holiday walk or gathering around an outdoor fire basket, you will be ready to sip a cup of wassail or other liquor-laced wintertime punch.

Christmas is a magical time with an intricate and centuries-old history, and details from that fascinating past are woven throughout this book. So as you select the dishes for your holiday menu, read about their origins and you will enjoy your Downton Christmas even more.

INGREDIENTS

Here are some ingredient guidelines to make using this book easier and to ensure greater success when making the recipes.

DAIRY AND EGGS

Butter: All butter is unsalted and must contain a minimum of 80 percent butterfat. (This is the minimum required by law for any product labeled "butter" in the United States.) Butter sold in Europe and so-called European-style butters sold in the United States have a higher butterfat content, usually 82 to 86 percent.

Buttermilk: In the past, buttermilk was the liquid left behind after churning butter, but today

most buttermilk is cultured milk. Both low-fat and whole-milk buttermilk are available, though the former is typically easier to find. Either can be used for this book. Buttermilk is usually stocked near the yogurt aisle in supermarkets.

Cream: Always use heavy cream (UK double cream), sometimes labeled "heavy whipping cream," in the recipes. The most commonly available heavy cream contains 36 to 38 percent butterfat. A cream with at least 40 percent butterfat is ideal for the recipes in this book, though it will require a search of smaller producers in the United States. (Double cream contains about 48 percent butterfat.) Pass up cream labeled "whipping cream," which has a much lower butterfat content.

Eggs: Use large (UK medium) eggs, preferably organic. Good-quality eggs will give your cakes and other baked goods volume, structure, flavor, and richness, and their yolks will impart color.

Milk: All milk is whole, or full-fat, milk. I find that skimmed milk does not yield the same satisfying result in terms of mouthfeel, flavor, and texture. In some cases, the lower butterfat will also adversely affect the baking or cooking process.

FATS

Lard: The rendered fat of a pig, lard has the advantage of both a high smoke point and a distinctive flavor. It was regularly favored in the past for frying and for the hot water pastry used in the making of traditional savory pies. For the

best result, purchase nonhydrogenated, naturally processed lard free of preservatives. You can also make your own lard by rendering pork fat at home. Just ask your butcher for either leaf fat, which produces a whiter, more refined lard, or fatback, which yields a more rustic lard. Cut it into small, uniform pieces, very slowly render it over low heat, strain to remove any impurities, and store in an airtight container in the refrigerator for a few months or in the freezer for up to a year.

Suet: This is kidney fat, usually obtained only from beef nowadays, though mutton was also used in the past. The best-selling beef suet brand in the United Kingdom is Atora, which packages it already shredded. Atora suet is widely available online and in some markets in the United States. In a pinch, grated frozen butter can be substituted.

FLAVORINGS AND SWEETENERS

Apricot kernels: Today, almond extract is used in desserts in place of the bitter almonds called for in the past. Nor can you even try to make the recipes the old way. Bitter almonds naturally contain high amounts of a cyanide precursor, so their sale is banned in many countries, including the United States and Britain. (Although pure almond extract is made from bitter almonds, the toxicity is eliminated in the manufacturing of the product.) But you can get closer to the original flavor by using skinned sweet apricot kernels. Like bitter almonds, sweet apricot kernels contain a cyanide precursor, but the level is much lower, which makes them safe to consume in the quantities used in the recipes. Keep unused apricot kernels packed in a well-labeled jar so no roommate, spouse, or peckish teenager starts snacking on them.

Candied citrus peel: Good-quality candied orange and lemon peel strips are ¼ inch (6 mm) thick or thicker. The skin must be sticky, and the strips should appear juicy. Pass up any that look dry or are marred by cracks.

Currants and raisins: Select dried currants and dark and golden raisins (UK sultanas) that have good color and appear neither crystallized nor dry. When adding them to cakes or fruit loaves, it is always best not to soak them in advance. If you add plump soaked fruits to a dough, they can get damaged during the final kneading or shaping process, and if you add them to a dough at an early stage, they can introduce unwanted moisture. I prefer to work with a wetter dough that compensates for the fact the fruit is not soaked. The fruit also attaches better to the framework of the baked good when using this method.

Golden syrup and black treacle: These are by-products of sugar refining and are typically English. Lyle's brand golden syrup, the best-known English maker, is available in some grocery stores and online in the United States, though it can be replaced by high-quality maple syrup or honey if you've failed to plan ahead. Lyle's also markets black treacle, though it is more difficult to find outside of the United Kingdom. Light or medium (dark) molasses is a good substitute.

Herbs: A variety of fresh herbs, such as parsley, thyme, marjoram, sage, savory, chervil, and mint, are called for, all of which Mrs. Patmore would have used freshly harvested from the estate garden. In the case of bay leaf, I have specified fresh bay when it is preferred over dried.

Salt: I used fine sea salt in all the recipes, but feel free to use whatever you have on hand, as long as the crystals are not too large or rough and thus hard to absorb or dissolve.

Spices: Purchase your spices in small quantities if possible, as their flavor diminishes over time, especially when forgotten at the back of a cupboard and rediscovered only after three years. If a recipe calls for many different spices and assembling them all seems too daunting, you can sometimes use mixed spice, a popular UK blend of sweet spices (typically nutmeg, cinnamon, allspice, cloves, coriander, and ginger); pumpkin pie spice, a similar blend widely sold in the United States; or chai spice mix in their place. The substitution will not yield the same taste, but the result will still be very good.

Sugar: A handful of sugars are used in this book. When I call for "sugar," I mean plain granulated sugar. Superfine (UK caster) sugar, confectioners' (UK icing) sugar, light and dark brown sugar, and Demerara, a pale amber, large-grain, minimally refined sugar, are also used.

Vanilla: Both the seeds of a vanilla bean (UK pod) and pure vanilla extract (UK essence) are called for in this book, the latter as an alternative to the more traditional mace and bay in the Custard Sauce on page 155.

FLOURS AND LEAVENERS

Baking powder: This common leavener is activated when exposed to moisture or heat. In contrast to baking soda (UK bicarbonate of soda), which is made of only sodium bicarbonate, baking powder contains sodium bicarbonate, two acids, and usually cornstarch (UK corn flour) to keep the mixture dry. In the past, baking powder was single acting, and a batter had to be baked quickly once liquid was introduced. But nowadays nearly all baking powder is double acting (made possible by the two acids), which gives the baker a little more time to get the batter in the oven. Store baking powder in a cool, dry place and make sure it has not sat on the shelf too long, as it loses its leavening power when old.

Flours: When I call for flour, I am using all-purpose (UK plain) flour, which has a protein content of 9 to 11 percent and is generally ideal for cakes, pastries, sauces, and the like. Bread (UK strong white) flour has a higher protein content of 11 to 13 percent, which yields a more elastic dough with a better rise. I also call for semolina flour, made from durum wheat, for the spinach balls on page 144 and for rice flour, finely milled from white rice, for both savory and sweet recipes.

Yeast: Although Mrs. Patmore would have used fresh yeast, active dry yeast is of great quality these days, so I use it. If you prefer fresh yeast, you will need to use about two and a half times more fresh yeast by weight than active dry yeast (1 teaspoon active dry yeast is 4 g).

MEAT AND POULTRY

If your budget permits, purchase meat and poultry that have been sustainably raised and with the animals' welfare topmost in mind. This varies from species to species and can mean everything from cage-free chickens to pasture-raised beef and lamb to free-range pork. It is both the most responsible way to shop and what would have been available to the kitchen staff at Downton. Remember, too, it's Christmas, so you may want to fast from meat and poultry for a month and then splurge on the very best bird or beef roast you can find!

If you are vegetarian or vegan, I apologize for the paucity of options in the following pages, but the mission of this book is to reflect the food on the table of the Crawleys. Although cookery books about vegetarian food and vegetables were available at the time, that type of cooking would not have reached an aristocratic household like Downton, especially one where the surrounding countryside offered so much game.

EQUIPMENT

The average outfitted kitchen will have the cookware, bakeware, and tools needed for making nearly every recipe in this book. The notable exception is the game meat mold for the Yorkshire Christmas Pie on page 113. In other cases, if you lack a specific cooking vessel, an easy fix is almost always possible. For example, you can substitute heatproof bowls of roughly equal size for pudding molds (basins).

For the ice cream recipes, I've provided methods that require no machine, and for most of the batters and doughs, I have given hand methods, making them just as Mrs. Patmore would have made them. But you are welcome to use an ice cream maker, stand or handheld mixer, and food processor for ease. Two inexpensive kitchen tools I consider essential are an oven thermometer and an instant-read thermometer. Too often ovens do not heat to the set temperature, so using the thermometer will allow you to adjust the setting mechanism to ensure the oven is at the correct temperature. (If you have a convection oven, never turn the fan on when using the recipes in this book.) An instant-read thermometer is indispensable for checking doneness for everything from your holiday turkey to a meat pie.

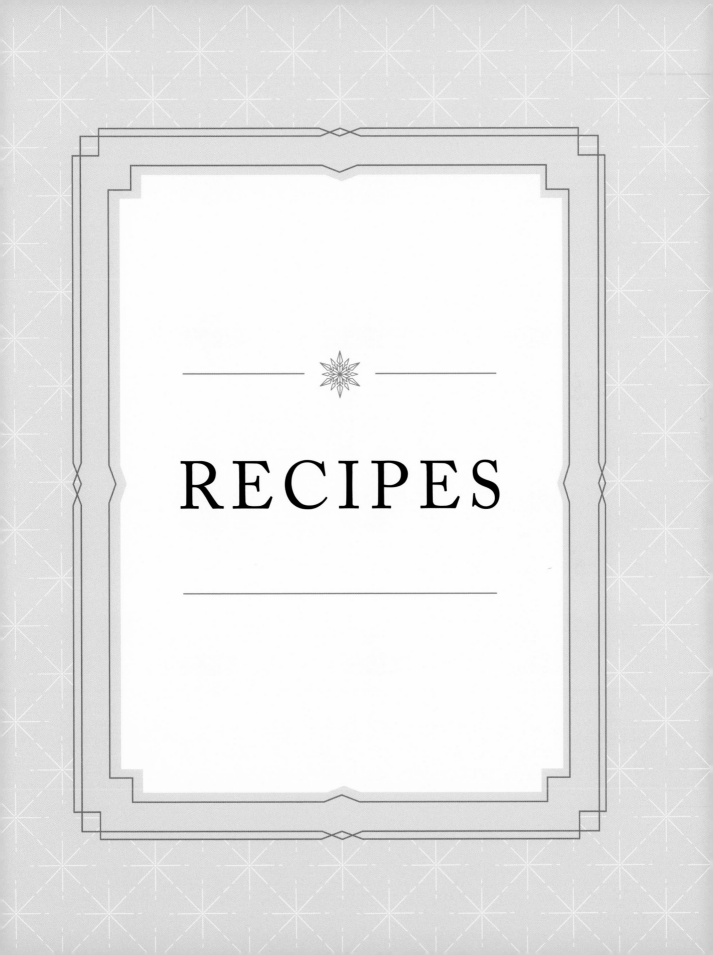

RECIPES

MRS. BIRD

What have you done with this [soup], you little beggar? I knew it.
That's why I said it was for upstairs. Come on. Tell us what's in it!

DAISY

Just water and a bit of soap.

~ SEASON 1, EPISODE 7

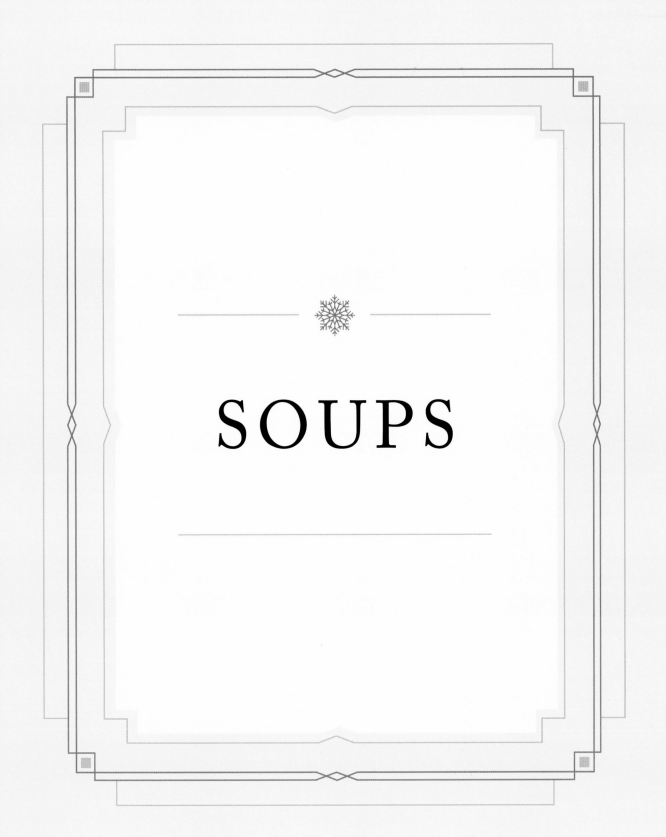

SOUPS

PHEASANT SOUP

In *Good Things in England,* a cookery book published in 1932 with recipes dating back to the fourteenth century, author Florence White includes this recipe in her menu for December. Other recipe books from the period suggest using "grandpapa" birds for this soup because they are too tough for the table but perfect for soup. When hunting parties at Downton went out for the day, they could not know from a distance if the pheasants were young or old, so the older birds would become soup and forcemeat while the young ones could be roasted whole or filleted for use in pies.

While balls of forcemeat are fine, quenelles are particularly striking when nicely placed in the soup plate with the celery and the clear stock ladled around them. If you cannot find a pheasant easily, a chicken can be used for both the stock and the quenelles.

SERVES 6

INGREDIENTS

1 large pheasant or chicken, about 3½ lb (1.6 kg)

6½ tablespoons (100 ml) sherry

FOR THE MIREPOIX

1 carrot, peeled and roughly chopped

1 yellow onion, quartered

1 rib celery, roughly chopped

1 leek, white and pale green parts, roughly chopped

1 clove garlic, crushed

5 black peppercorns

¼ teaspoon salt

Bouquet garni of 2 fresh flat-leaf parsley sprigs, 2 fresh thyme sprigs, and 1 bay leaf, tied into a bundle with kitchen string

2 quarts (2 l) water

FOR THE QUENELLES

Reserved pheasant breast fillets

¼ cup (30 g) flour

1 egg yolk

1 tablespoon finely chopped fresh flat-leaf parsley

⅛ teaspoon salt

⅛ teaspoon black pepper

2 cups (475 ml) chicken stock

FOR GARNISH

1 large, thick rib celery

Finely chopped fresh flat-leaf parsley

Using a sharp knife, cut the breast fillets off the pheasant and refrigerate for making the quenelles. Leave the remaining meat on the carcass. Using a cleaver or heavy knife, break the legs to make the carcass more manageable inside the pot. Put the carcass into a large, deep pot and add all the mirepoix ingredients, the bouquet garni, and the water, adding more water if needed just to cover. Bring to a boil over high heat, skimming off any foam that forms on the surface. Reduce the heat to medium-low and simmer gently, skimming off any foam that forms and adding water as needed to maintain the original level, for 3 hours.

When the stock is ready, remove from the heat and pass through a fine-mesh sieve placed over a saucepan. You will be left with a great stock that will be the base for your soup. If you are using a young bird, remove the meat from the legs, tear it into small bite-size pieces, and add it to the stock. Reserve the stock for adding just before serving.

Recipe continues

While the stock is bubbling away, make the quenelles. Remove the skin from the pheasant breasts and discard. You should have 14 oz (400 g) flesh. Cut the flesh into 1-inch (2.5-cm) chunks, arrange in a single layer on a small sheet pan, and freeze for 20 minutes. Working in two or three batches, add the pheasant chunks to a food processor and pulse just until ground. As each batch is ground, transfer it to a bowl.

Add the flour, egg yolk, parsley, salt, and pepper to the ground pheasant and mix gently but thoroughly to form a cohesive forcemeat. To shape the quenelles, using 2 soupspoons with deep bowls, scoop up a generous amount of the pheasant mixture in 1 spoon, gently press the bowl of the second spoon against the forcemeat to smooth the surface and shape the top, and then ease the quenelle off the first spoon onto a flat plate. Repeat with the remaining forcemeat. You should have 18 quenelles. Alternatively, roll the forcemeat between your palms to make small balls about 1 inch (2.5 cm) in diameter (the meatballs are better smaller and you will have twice as many).

Pour the chicken stock into a saucepan and bring to a boil over medium heat. Using a slotted spoon or wire skimmer, carefully lower the quenelles into the stock and boil gently until cooked through, 4–5 minutes. Scoop the quenelles out of the stock into a bowl, cover, and keep warm. (Discard the stock or reserve for another use.)

To make the garnish, using a small melon baller, cut out at least 60 balls from the thick part of the celery rib. If the celery rib is too thin for carving out balls, or if you don't have a small melon baller, cut the celery into neat ½-inch (12-mm) cubes.

When ready to serve, warm 6 soup plates. Bring the strained pheasant stock to a boil, add the sherry, and transfer to a tureen. Place a few celery "peas" or cubes and 3 warm quenelles in each warmed soup plate and sprinkle with a little parsley. Set a soup plate on the table in front of each guest, then go around the table and ladle the stock around the quenelles and celery garnish.

RECIPE NOTE

Ask your butcher for pheasant or chicken carcasses (they are often free). Also request your butcher to joint the pheasant and weigh the fillets; you'll need about 14 oz (400 g) of meat for the quenelles. If necessary, purchase an extra fillet or minced chicken to reach the weight.

PALESTINE SOUP

Downton Abbey starts in the Edwardian era, when the range of foods eaten, especially vegetables, was greater than today, and there was a particular vogue for root vegetables. This soup, which was ubiquitous on Edwardian Christmas menus, gets its name, Palestine, from the inclusion of what are known in Britain as Jerusalem artichokes (sunchokes), though there is no real link to the actual region.

SERVES 6

RECIPE NOTE

This soup can be made with other starchy vegetables, such as potato, winter squash, parsnip, and salsify, an Edwardian favorite. You can also vary the seasonings, swapping out the cayenne for curry powder or the parsley for sage, for example.

INGREDIENTS

2 lb (I kg) Jerusalem artichokes, cut into ½-inch (12-mm) pieces

I small turnip, peeled and cut into ½-inch (12-mm) pieces

I yellow onion, chopped

3 ribs celery, chopped

4 cups (950 ml) chicken or veal stock

2 teaspoons cayenne pepper

Scant I teaspoon salt

½ teaspoon sugar

Black pepper

½ cup (120 ml) heavy cream (preferably at least 40 percent butterfat)

FOR THE CROUTONS AND FRIED PARSLEY

4 thin slices white bread

I–2 tablespoons unsalted butter, or as needed, for frying

I small bunch fresh flat-leaf parsley, large stems discarded, finely chopped

Combine the Jerusalem artichokes, turnip, onion, celery, stock, cayenne, salt, sugar, and a little black pepper in a large saucepan and bring to a boil over high heat. Reduce the heat to a simmer, cover partially, and simmer until the vegetables are tender, about I hour.

Meanwhile, make the croutons and fried parsley. Using a small biscuit or cookie cutter, cut the bread into shapes. (Stars, diamonds, and triangles are all suitably Edwardian.) In a frying pan, melt the butter over medium heat. When it foams, add the bread cutouts and fry, turning as needed to color evenly, until golden brown on all sides, 3–5 minutes. Transfer the cutouts to a bowl. Add the parsley to the same pan and fry over medium heat until just crispy, about I minute, adding more butter as needed. Transfer to a separate bowl.

When the vegetables are tender, remove the pan from the heat and let the soup cool slightly. Working in batches, transfer the soup to a blender and purée until smooth. Transfer the puréed soup to a clean saucepan and reheat over gentle heat, stirring often, to serving temperature. Stir in the cream and heat through.

Ladle the soup into warmed bowls, dot with the croutons and fried parsley, and serve hot. Or offer the croutons and parsley on the side for diners to help themselves.

RECIPE NOTE

Although at Downton the soup would have been served by a footman from a tureen, it is very pretty offered already plated and garnished with a mixture of wild mushrooms, fried and kept warm; a scattering of chopped fresh flat-leaf parsley; and a drizzle of truffle oil. Sippets, the small triangle toasts served with Baked John Dory (page 56), are also a nice accompaniment.

CREAM OF MUSHROOM SOUP

Mrs. C. F. Leyel and Miss Olga Hartley published their delightful *The Gentle Art of Cookery*, from which this recipe comes, in 1925. On mushrooms, the authors write that if red mullet are the woodcocks of the sea because of their delicate taste, then mushrooms might be called the oysters of the fields, for no other food has the same rare flavor of these elfin-like mysteries that grow by the light of the moon, or, more accurately, in darkness.

The traditional way to prepare this soup is to make a roux and then mix it with stock and cream. The flavor is earthy and warming, and the soup becomes extra luxurious and ideal for Christmas with a drizzle of truffle oil once plated. Truffle was a popular—and costly—addition to dishes in Victorian times and would have been used in the Downton era. But truffle oil was not yet available except in Italian and French kitchens, where chefs made their own. So Mrs. Patmore would have used truffle shavings for this soup, if she could get her hands on some. If possible, use brown mushrooms, also known as cremini, Italian brown, or Roman mushrooms, which will yield a more flavorful soup than white mushrooms.

SERVES 6

INGREDIENTS

5 cups (1.2 l) vegetable or chicken stock

3 tablespoons unsalted butter

2 shallots, minced

9 oz (250 g) brown mushrooms or 18 oz (500 g) white mushrooms, brushed clean and thinly sliced

Salt and black pepper

2 tablespoons flour

1 cup (240 ml) heavy cream (preferably at least 40 percent butterfat)

⅓ cup (80 ml) Sauternes

Bring the stock to a gentle simmer in a saucepan over medium-low heat. Melt 1 tablespoon of the butter in a heavy sauté pan over medium heat. Add the shallots and mushrooms and cook, stirring continuously to make sure they don't stick to the pan, until the mushrooms are browned, 12–15 minutes. Add a pinch of salt and 2 pinches of pepper and stir well. Pour in 1 cup (240 ml) of the hot stock and deglaze the pan, stirring to scrape up any browned bits from the pan bottom. Set the pan aside off the heat.

In a pot large enough to hold the soup once it is fully assembled, melt the remaining 2 tablespoons butter over medium heat. Add the flour and immediately stir with a wooden spoon until well mixed. Reduce the heat to low and continue to stir until the mixture comes together as a roux. It is ready when the aroma changes from butter and raw flour to the scent of baked biscuits. You will notice a more nutty smell and the color will darken to a light fudge shade. Remove the pot from the heat and slowly pour in 1 cup (240 ml) of the stock, stirring constantly to prevent lumps from forming. (If some lumps form, use a handheld mixer to beat the mixture until smooth.) Return the pan to medium heat and slowly add the remaining hot stock, a little at a time, while stirring continuously. When all of the stock is incorporated, stir in the cream and bring to a simmer. Season with salt and pepper. Finally, pour in the Sauternes, stir well, and let cool slightly.

Scoop out 4–5 tablespoons (30 g) cooked mushrooms and reserve. Add the remaining cooked mushrooms to the soup pot and stir well. Working in batches, transfer the soup to a blender and blend until smooth. Transfer the puréed soup to a clean saucepan and reheat over gentle heat, stirring often, to serving temperature, then stir in the reserved mushrooms.

Ladle the soup into warmed bowls and serve immediately.

HOW TO HOST A DOWNTON CHRISTMAS

Part of the charm of Christmas is all the preparations: selecting the proper gifts, decorating with evergreens and flowers, putting up a tree, planning the menu and the entertainment. Then, come Christmas Eve, everything is perfect. Nowadays, many of us begin decorating the house a week or two before Christmas, with some perhaps beginning as early as Advent Sunday (the fourth Sunday before Christmas Day). In the Edwardian period and into the 1920s, decorating would start on December 24. Of course, much would need to be prepared ahead of this day so everything was ready to go.

To transform your dining room into a Christmas of yesteryear, begin with greenery. Arrange an abundance of winter greens down the middle of the dining table, on side tables, and even in a fireplace that will remain unlit. Fashion a garland of evergreens and drape it on and around the mantelpiece. You can be extravagant with these decorations, as there's no such thing as "less is more" with evergreens at holiday time. Even though Downton Abbey had electricity, candles were always on the table for the Christmas feast, bathing both the food and the diners in a warm, inviting glow that people still welcome today. Taper candles are a good choice. Choose unscented ones, preferably of beeswax, which has a nearly undetectable naturally sweet scent and burns both slowly and cleanly.

The Christmas tree at Downton is set up in the great hall, but putting your tree in the dining room or in the area where you will be serving drinks before the meal would add to the festive ambience of your holiday dinner. Either of these two places is also where people in the Downton era not living on a splendid English estate would have most often placed it and where many people today set it up.

CREATING DECORATIONS

Gather your evergreens, such as holly, ivy, bay or laurel, fir branches, and/or rosemary, a few days ahead of Christmas. Pine cones are a great addition, as are branches of *Ilex verticillata* (winterberry holly), with their bright (inedible) red berries. If you live in a city, you can find beautiful winter greens at florist shops during the Christmas season, or you can head to your local park and, if permitted, collect some windfall leaves and small branches and maybe a pine cone or two. Walnuts, hazelnuts, chestnuts, apples, and pears are also nice additions. So, too, are oranges spiked with cloves, which give off a wonderful festive scent.

To create a garland for decorating a mantelpiece or even a bookcase or window, you will need some twine and a pair of sturdy garden scissors. Long trails of holly or various vines, such as plants of the *Parthenocissus* genus (Boston ivy and other climbing members of the grape family), can serve as the base. Bind together a couple of long trails to achieve the length needed for your garland, twisting them around each other to create a good base for tying on lots of other greens. You want your finished garland to look abundant. If you're not up to a bit of flower crafting—though simple bouquets of unscented white roses or other white flowers are always nice—you can fill a number of vases of different sizes with greens and then cluster them together to give a look of luxury. Arrangements of both flowers and greens with a bit of height were very much favored in the Downton era. If you have tall glass vases that resemble oversized wineglasses, this is the place to use them.

Of course, such bountiful foliage displays would not have been seen in working-class homes in the Edwardian period. But people found simple yet still lovely ways to dress up their houses. Paper chains were popular, often made in a variety of colors by children in the family. You need only scissors, construction paper in different colors, and a glue stick, double-sided tape, or a stapler (in the past, a homemade paste of flour and water would serve as the glue) to make these charming chains: First cut uniform strips of paper. Strips about eight inches (20 cm) long and one inch (2.5 cm) wide are a good size. Glue, tape, or staple one strip into a ring, making sure it is secure. Then thread a second strip through the ring and secure it the same way. The two links should sit at a rough 90-degree angle. Continue to add links until you have a chain the length you want.

BEFORE DINNER

In the era Downton is set, it was common to have a Christmas drink before going through to dinner, which was always held in another room. In the series, the staff and guests are seen enjoying cups of wassail, but cocktails were also incredibly popular in the stylish 1920s. For an authentic feel of the period, you can prepare Wassail and serve it from a large punch bowl that has matching cups. If you opt instead for cocktails, they should be already prepared and on a tray when the guests arrive.

At Downton Abbey, this would also be the time to sing a holiday carol and propose a toast. Then, when it was time to continue on to the dining room, the host would accompany the woman with the highest status—today that might be his mother—and the hostess would accompany the man with the highest status—today perhaps her father. Of course, it is also fine to dispense with concerns about status and go through to dinner in whatever pairings are comfortable for everyone.

THE MENU

Eight courses were the standard for a holiday meal at aristocratic households of the era. But it is better to focus on three or four courses and perhaps a small savory with the before-dinner drink than to commit to preparing a feast that would require the help of Daisy and footmen. No food would be on the table, apart from a bowl of fruit or nuts. That means no showing off of that perfectly roasted goose or turkey and then carving it at the table for all to see, as is often done today. Instead, footmen would present you with the choice of foods for your selection. As you likely won't have your own Thomas, it is a good idea to have a side table where the dishes are displayed. You can then plate the food there and place it in front of each guest. That way everyone gets to see the all-important roast meat.

The courses might be a soup; a fish starter; a showstopper roast or, if the party is small, one of the more modest meat dishes; a choice of two or three vegetable dishes; and then a selection of desserts, with one of them Christmas pudding. Finally, offer a choice of two or three savories, small dishes much like the *amuse-bouches* served today at the beginning of a meal. These savories were also what the Crawley family would traditionally have for their Christmas Day lunch, serving themselves while the staff was having its Christmas dinner downstairs. This custom of the upstairs family making do without staff was highly unusual for the period, but it was a tradition at Downton—one that surprised Mary's suitor in season 2, as is evident in the following exchange: "But why can't they have their lunch early and then serve us, like they normally do?" asks Carlisle. "Because it's Christmas Day," responds Mary.

SETTING THE TABLE

A crisp, white tablecloth and starched white napkins (or perhaps colored ones) are obligatory. The napkins, which often concealed a bread roll on the aristocratic table, are placed on bread plates that sit to the upper left of the dinner plate. You'll need a set of cutlery for each course and four glasses—footed glass for water, white wine, red wine, and dessert wine—which are arranged to the upper right of the dinner plate. The final element is a handwritten menu in a menu-card holder positioned above the dinner plate and next to the glasses.

To create handwritten menus for your holiday dinner, purchase some textured white paper at an art-supply store (buy a little extra in case you make an error while writing) and cut the paper to a size that will accommodate the listing of all the dishes without crowding. If you own a calligraphy pen, use it, but you can buy brush pens these days that work well, too. Use a soapstone pencil to draw lines—you will need as many lines as you have dishes, plus one for the word *menu* at the top—on each menu card, then write the dishes on the cards. Let the ink dry completely before carefully erasing the pencil lines.

OXTAIL CONSOMMÉ

Oxtail is an especially delicious cut of meat if given time to cook slowly in a bath of stock or wine. When done, the meat readily falls from the bone and is fork-tender and deeply flavorful. Oxtail is often sold already cut into pieces about 1½ inches (4 cm) long. Make sure the butcher gives you meaty pieces. If it is not already cut, use a sharp knife to cut the tail between the joints.

The recipe for oxtail soup in *Mrs Beeton's Book of Household Management* calls for bringing the oxtail to a boil in a pot of water and then discarding the water before adding all the remaining soup ingredients. That step is unnecessary and has been skipped here. Mrs. Beeton also instructs the cook to clarify the stock and serve it as a consommé. But properly clarifying a stock is time-consuming and wasteful in today's world, so the choice as to whether to clarify or not has been left to you. If you skip the step, this will not be a true consommé, but it will still be lovely.

SERVES 6

INGREDIENTS

2 lb (1 kg) oxtail, cut between the joints into pieces about 1½ inches (4 cm) long

Flour, for dusting

Unsalted butter, for frying

1 yellow onion, chopped

1 rib celery, chopped

½ turnip, chopped

Bouquet garni of 2 fresh flat-leaf parsley sprigs, 2 fresh thyme sprigs, and 1 bay leaf, tied into a bundle with kitchen string

6 black peppercorns

2 whole cloves

1 blade mace

2 quarts (2 l) beef or vegetable stock

FOR SERVING

1 turnip, peeled and cut into ¼-inch (6-mm) cubes

1 carrot, peeled and cut into ¼-inch (6-mm) cubes

½ cup (120 ml) sherry

Salt and black pepper

Lightly dust the oxtail pieces with flour. In a Dutch oven or other heavy pot, melt 1 tablespoon butter over medium heat. Working in batches to avoid crowding, add the oxtail pieces and lightly brown on all sides, 5–7 minutes for each batch, adding an additional 1 tablespoon butter each batch. As the batches are ready, transfer them to a plate.

Return the oxtail pieces to the pot, add the onion, celery, turnip, bouquet garni, peppercorns, cloves, and mace, and pour in the stock. Cover and bring to a boil over medium heat. Reduce the heat to medium-low and simmer, covered, until the meat falls from the bone when nudged with a fork, 2½–3 hours. Alternatively, bring to a boil on the stove top as directed, then place the covered pot in a preheated 325°F (165°C) oven and braise the oxtail pieces for 2½ hours. At this point, check to see if the meat is falling from the bone. If it is not, return the pot to the oven and check again after 30 minutes.

When the oxtail is ready, using a slotted spoon, transfer the pieces to a sheet pan. Strain the contents of the pot through a fine-mesh sieve set over a bowl or other container and discard the solids. Let the stock cool. Cover the meat and the stock and refrigerate overnight.

The next day, scoop off any fat that has hardened on the surface of the stock. If clarifying the stock, follow the directions that follow. Pick the meat from the bones, tear larger pieces into small bite-size chunks. and set aside.

To serve, pour the stock into a saucepan, add the turnip and carrot cubes, and bring to a boil over high heat. Add the reserved meat and the sherry and heat just until the meat is hot. Season with salt and pepper. Ladle into warmed bowls and serve.

TO CLARIFY THE STOCK

You will need to use ground beef, egg whites, and vegetables for this step, all of which you then throw away. Thus, it is a costly process and one that would only have been done for the tables of grand houses like Downton. It is important to season the stock before you clarify it, as the addition of pepper can cloud it.

3½ oz (100 g) ground beef	2 fresh bay leaves
½ carrot, roughly chopped	Pinch of salt
I rib celery, roughly chopped	Pinch of black pepper
2½ tablespoons tomato paste	3 egg whites

In a blender or food processor, combine the beef, carrot, celery, tomato paste, bay leaves, salt, and pepper. Pour the egg whites over the top and process until smooth.

In a saucepan, heat the stock over medium heat until hot. Add the egg white mixture to the hot stock and, with the pan still over medium heat, bring the stock to a boil, then adjust the heat to maintain a simmer. The egg white "raft" will solidify and catch all the impurities in the stock. Let the stock simmer for 20 minutes while the egg whites do their job.

MRS. PATMORE: *Ooh talk about making a silk purse out of a sow's ear. I wish we had a sow's ear. It'd be better than this brisket.*

~ SEASON 2, EPISODE 7

Line a fine-mesh sieve with cheesecloth and set it over a clean saucepan. Pass the stock through the sieve and discard the contents of the sieve. Proceed as directed in the recipe to serve the soup.

VIOLET
Is it a long list, Lord Sinderby? The things you disapprove of?

SINDERBY
*No. As long as I can steer clear of card sharps and
undercooked fish and divorce, I think I'm fairly easy.*

~ SEASON 5, EPISODE 8

FISH & SHELLFISH

BAKED JOHN DORY

Stewed cucumbers were the traditional garnish for this dish, but thinly sliced fresh cucumber is a superior choice and looks particularly striking. The triangular croutons, which were called "sippets" in historical recipes, have been served with savory dishes of all kinds—soups, broths, meats, fish—since the thirteenth century. It might seem strange to contemporary diners to serve toast with fish, but it is a surprisingly pleasant pairing.

SERVES 4

INGREDIENTS

FOR THE FISH

Unsalted butter, for the baking dish

4 skin-on John Dory or petrale sole fillets, about ½ lb (225 g) each

1 bunch fresh chives

1 bunch fresh chervil

1 bunch fresh flat-leaf parsley

1 egg, lightly beaten

Salt and black pepper

¼ cup (60 ml) fish stock

2 tablespoons dry white wine

FOR THE CROUTONS

3–4 thin slices white bread

1 tablespoon unsalted butter

FOR THE SAUCE

1 tablespoon unsalted butter

1 tablespoon flour

⅔ cup (160 ml) fish stock

1 anchovy fillet in olive oil, minced

Juice of ¼ lemon

Salt and black pepper

½ cucumber, peeled, if desired, and thinly sliced, for garnish

Chopped fresh flat-leaf parsley, chives, and/or chervil, for garnish (optional)

To prepare the fish, preheat the oven to 400°F (200°C). Butter a baking dish just large enough to accommodate the fish fillets in two layers.

Chop the chives, chervil, and parsley roughly, discarding any coarse stems, then toss together in a small bowl. Brush the fish fillets all over with the beaten egg and season them with salt and pepper.

Scatter one-third of the mixed herbs over the bottom of the prepared baking dish and place 2 fillets, skin side down, on top. Sprinkle the flesh side of the fillets in the dish with the remaining mixed herbs, coating them evenly. Place the remaining 2 fillets, skin side up, on top of the fillets in the dish, so the herbs are sandwiched between the two layers of fillets. In a small cup or bowl, stir together the stock and wine, then pour the mixture into the dish.

Bake the fish just until it flakes when tested with a fork, 10–15 minutes.

Recipe continues

While the fish bakes, make the croutons. Cut each bread slice into 4 neat triangles. Melt the butter in a large ovenproof frying pan over medium heat. Add the triangles and fry, turning as needed, until golden brown on both sides, about 5 minutes. Set the croutons aside in the pan.

When the fish is ready, remove from the oven and spoon out the liquid from the dish into a small bowl. Keep the fish warm and leave the oven on.

To make the sauce, melt the butter in a small saucepan over medium heat. Add the flour and whisk until smooth. Reduce the heat to low and stir constantly for 1–2 minutes to cook off the raw flour taste. Add the stock little by little, stirring constantly to prevent any lumps from forming. Continue to stir until the mixture is smooth and thickens slightly. Stir in the anchovy and lemon juice, then add the reserved liquid from the baking dish and stir well. Raise the heat to medium and bring to a simmer, stirring constantly. Season to taste with salt and pepper. Remove from the heat and keep warm.

Slip the pan with the croutons into the oven to warm while you assemble the dish. Arrange the fillets, skin side down, on a warmed oval serving plate and decorate them with the cucumber slices. Pour the sauce around the fillets, then garnish the plate with herbs, if using. Retrieve the croutons from the oven, arrange them around the rim of the plate, and serve.

MRS. HUGHES: *Anything could happen for you, it's a wonderful feeling.*

DAISY: *Maybe.*

MRS. PATMORE: *And if it means a bit of extra work for me, so be it. And happy Christmas.*

~ SEASON 5, EPISODE 9

RISSOLES OF SALMON

Sport fishing was nearly as popular as hunting with the upper classes, as we see in the final episode of season 3, when almost the entire Crawley family goes to Duneagle castle in the river-rich Scottish Highlands to visit Susan, the niece of the Dowager Countess; her husband, Shrimpie MacClare; and their free-spirited daughter, Lady Rose. Salmon was particularly abundant in Scottish rivers in the Downton era, and it was used in a variety of celebration-worthy dishes, from whole fish elaborately decorated or in aspic to these festive rissoles.

A popular first course, rissoles were made in various ways: as round puff-pastry packets, as in this recipe; as cannelons, or stuffed pastry rolls; and as croquettes. The filling could range from rice to ground or pounded meat, chicken, or fish. In her highly regarded best-seller *Modern Cookery*, first published in 1845, Eliza Acton gives several options, including Potato Rissoles (French) and Very Savoury English Rissoles. She instructs the cook to apply an egg wash and then add a layer of bread crumbs or finely broken vermicelli; the first is a particularly nice addition.

SERVES 4 AS A FIRST COURSE

INGREDIENTS

Flour, for the work surface

18 oz (500 g) all-butter puff pastry, thawed according to package directions if frozen

1 skinless salmon fillet, 9 oz (250 g) and no more than ¾ inch (2 cm) thick

2 fresh dill sprigs, finely chopped

4 teaspoons unsalted butter

1 egg yolk, beaten

1 tablespoon dried bread crumbs

Preheat the oven 425°F (220°C). Line a sheet pan with parchment paper.

On a lightly floured work surface, roll out the puff pastry a scant ¼ inch (6 mm) thick. Using a 4½-inch (11.5-cm) round pastry cutter, cut out 8 rounds. Lift away the extra pastry.

Cut the salmon into 4 equal pieces, making sure each piece will fit in the center of a pastry round surrounded by a 1-inch (2.5-cm) border. Top 4 of the pastry rounds with a piece of salmon. Sprinkle the dill over the salmon pieces, dividing it evenly, then top each piece with 1 teaspoon of the butter. Brush the edge of each salmon-topped pastry round with a little of the egg yolk and top with the remaining pastry rounds. Seal the edges together well, crimping them with a thumb and index finger.

Brush the tops of the pastry packets with the egg yolk, then divide the bread crumbs evenly among the packets, sprinkling them onto the center. Carefully transfer the pastries to the prepared pan, spacing them well apart.

Bake the rissoles until the pastry is puffed, golden, and crisp, 20–25 minutes. Serve warm.

RECIPE NOTE

You can omit the bread crumb topping and instead decorate the packets with the pastry scraps left over from cutting out the rounds. Cut the scraps into decorative shapes—leaves were traditional, but stars or any other shape will do—and place the cutouts on the tops of the packets, pressing them gently to the egg yolk–brushed surface to adhere. Bake as directed.

SKATE AU VIN BLANC

Although quite simple in ingredients and to prepare, this dish turns out so pretty that it is sure to impress your guests. In the years immediately after World War I, the British—and especially British soldiers who had fought in Europe—were interested in eating more French, Italian, German, and even Dutch dishes. French food was considered especially fancy, including this dish with its chic French name. The recipe is adapted from one that appears in *The Gentle Art of Cookery* by C. F. Leyel and Olga Hartley, which featured many European-inspired dishes among its 750 recipes. Published in the mid-1920s, the volume, with its lighter cuisine, was embraced as a welcome change from the typically heavy, elaborately decorated dishes of Victorian and Edwardian kitchens.

SERVES 4

INGREDIENTS

Unsalted butter, for the sheet pan and the parchment

4 small skinned and boned skate wings, about ½ lb (225 g) each

FOR THE SAUCE

2 tablespoons unsalted butter

2 shallots, minced

4 white mushrooms, brushed clean and finely chopped

Salt and black pepper

1 tablespoon dried bread crumbs

1 cup (240 ml) dry white wine

3 tablespoons chopped fresh flat-leaf parsley

1 tablespoon chopped fresh basil or oregano

Preheat the oven to 400°F (200°C). Butter a sheet pan large enough to hold the skate wings in a single layer.

Place the skate wings on the prepared pan. Cut a sheet of parchment paper large enough to cover the fish, butter one side, and then place the parchment, buttered side down, over the fish. Bake the fish for 10–20 minutes; the timing will depend on how large and fat the skate wings are. When the flesh looks white and plump and lifts easily away from the cartilage, the wings are ready. If some translucent spots are visible, bake the fish a little longer.

While the fish bakes, make the sauce. Melt the butter in a saucepan over medium heat. Add the shallots and mushrooms and cook, stirring occasionally, until the shallots are translucent and the mushrooms are glazed, about 5 minutes. Do not allow them to color. Season with salt and pepper and stir in the bread crumbs, mixing well. Then pour in the wine, bring to a simmer, and simmer until the sauce thickens slightly, 5–8 minutes.

Remove the skate wings from the oven, lift off the parchment, and spoon out the buttery juices from the pan into the sauce. Return the sauce just to a simmer, remove from the heat, and stir in the parsley and basil.

Transfer the skate wings to a warmed serving dish or individual plates, spoon the sauce on and around them, and serve.

SOLE À LA DORCHESTER

Why this dish is called à la Dorchester is unknown (a variation made with tomato is titled à la Dorothea, again without explanation). It comes from Lady Agnes Jekyll's *Kitchen Essays*, first published in 1922. Jekyll mentions that when asparagus is no longer in season, peas can be used in its place. To serve this dish at Christmastime when asparagus (or even peas) was unavailable in the shops was a status symbol of the upper class—evidence that estate gardeners were able to force out-of-season produce to flourish in the coldest months of the year.

Lady Jekyll (née Graham) lived with her husband, Herbert, a respected public servant, and his sister Gertrude, an internationally recognized garden designer, artist, and writer. They were known for hosting dinner parties to which artists, art critics, and prominent social thinkers of the day were invited. Both women were outspoken and modern for their time, much like Lady Sybil and later Lady Edith, whose shared interest in art and social matters grows with the years.

SERVES 4 AS A MAIN COURSE OR 8 AS A FIRST COURSE

INGREDIENTS

20 green or white asparagus spears

Unsalted butter, for the baking dish

FOR THE BÉCHAMEL

2 tablespoons unsalted butter

⅓ cup (40 g) flour

3 cups (700 ml) whole milk

1 tablespoon grated Parmesan cheese

Salt and black pepper

8 skinless Dover sole fillets, 4–5 oz (115–140 g) each

2 tablespoons grated Parmesan cheese (optional)

Bend each asparagus toward the end of the stalk. The woody part should break off easily without wasting any of the tender part. Trim the ends so they are even, if needed. If using white asparagus, beginning just below the base of the tip, use a vegetable peeler to peel the length of the stalk, removing the fibrous skin. Green asparagus typically do not require peeling unless they are thick. Boil or steam the asparagus until fork-tender, then transfer them to a colander and hold under cold running water to halt the cooking. Drain well, then cut the stalks crosswise into ⅜-inch (1-cm) pieces and leave the tips whole.

Preheat the oven to 400°F (200°F). Butter a 2½-quart (2.5-l) baking dish or gratin dish.

To make the béchamel, melt the butter in a saucepan over medium heat. Add the flour and immediately stir with a wooden spoon until well mixed. Reduce the heat to low and continue to stir until the mixture is dry and comes together in a roux. It is ready when the aroma changes from butter and raw flour to the scent of baked biscuits and smells slighty nutty. Do not allow the mixture to color. Remove the pan from the heat and slowly pour in 1 cup (240 ml) of the milk, stirring constantly to prevent lumps from forming. (Removing the pan from the heat for this step ensures better control. If some lumps form, use a handheld mixer to beat the mixture until it is smooth.) Return the pan to medium-low heat and slowly add the remaining milk, a little at a time, while stirring continuously. When all of the milk has been incorporated, you should have a thick, smooth sauce. Stir in the Parmesan, season with salt and pepper, and remove from the heat.

If the sole fillets can be easily rolled, roll up each one and place it in the prepared dish. You might need to insert a wooden skewer to keep them rolled up, but do not forget to remove it before serving. If they cannot be easily rolled, lay them lengthwise in the prepared dish.

Toss the asparagus pieces into the béchamel and stir gently; reserve the asparagus tips for adding later. Pour the sauce evenly over and around the fish. Although Lady Jekyll does not suggest the addition, sprinkling a little Parmesan over the top improves the look of the finished dish.

Bake the fish just until it flakes when tested with a fork, 12–15 minutes. The timing will depend on the thickness of the fillets; if they were small, check at 10 minutes. Remove the dish from the oven and place the asparagus tips neatly around the edge of the dish in a manner that looks appealing and bake for 2 minutes longer. Serve warm.

RECIPE NOTE

Fillets of petrale, English, lemon, or rex sole can be substituted for the Dover sole; large fillets of plaice will also work.

MALAY CURRY OF PRAWNS

This recipe for curried prawns appears in Lady Agnes Jekyll's *Kitchen Essays* (see page 64). She includes it in the essay titled "Country Friends to a Christmas Luncheon" and suggests serving it to friends who are visiting London from the countryside to do their Christmas shopping. She notes that guests are particularly appreciative when the host takes the time to order ingredients (such as prawns and coconut milk) that aren't readily procurable outside the city.

Lady Jekyll isn't fond of all the hustle and bustle in London at Christmastime and writes amusingly both of her disapproval and of the need to invite friends to her table: "Country friends flock eagerly to town, armed with lists of things they are resolute to buy and bestow, and the offer of a house of rest, . . . and an agreeable luncheon will be an act of hospitality gratefully welcomed." She suggests this curry as an alternative to the more common oyster first course, describing it as capturing the true Eastern flavor for a Western palate. It would also make a lovely main course, increasing the prawns to six per serving.

SERVES 4 AS A FIRST COURSE

INGREDIENTS

16 head-on Tiger prawns or large shrimp in the shell, about 1½ lb (680 g) total	1 tablespoon rice flour
	1 teaspoon ground turmeric
Unsalted butter or olive oil, for cooking	1 teaspoon ground cinnamon
	1 teaspoon ground cloves
2 tablespoons Cognac, gin, or vodka	1 teaspoon Demerara sugar
¼ teaspoon cayenne pepper	¾ cup plus 2 tablespoons (200 ml) coconut milk
1 small yellow onion (the size of a golf ball), sliced into rings	1 cucumber, cut into ½-inch (12-mm) cubes
2 cloves garlic, chopped	Cooked white rice, for serving

Break off the heads of the prawns; peel the bodies, leaving the tail segments intact, then devein and set aside. Heat a knob of butter or splash of oil in a heavy frying pan over medium heat. Toss in the prawn heads and turn in the pan until they are bright red and some caramelization is visible on the pan bottom, about 5 minutes. Pour in the Cognac and deglaze the pan, dislodging any browned bits from the bottom. (The original recipe calls for simmering the prawn shells and heads in milk, but frying the heads and then deglazing the pan yields a more flavorful result.) Reduce the heat to low, stir in the cayenne pepper, and remove from the heat. Pour the contents of the pan through a fine-mesh sieve placed over a small bowl, then press against the heads with the back of a spoon to force through as much liquid as possible. Reserve the liquid.

Heat 1 tablespoon butter or oil in a large, shallow pan over medium heat. Add the onion and garlic and cook, stirring often, until the onion is golden, about 8 minutes. Add the flour, turmeric, cinnamon, and cloves and stir well so they get some heat. When the onion and spices start to caramelize slightly, stir in the sugar, mixing well, and then immediately pour in the prawn head liquid and coconut milk. Stir the sauce for 1 minute, then add the cucumber and simmer until the onion is soft, the sauce starts to thicken, and the cucumber has lost its crunch, about 10 minutes. Now add the shrimp and cook until they curl and are opaque, about 5 minutes longer.

To serve, divide the shrimp and sauce evenly among 4 plates and set the rice alongside.

VIOLET

A peer in favour of reform is like a turkey in favour of Christmas.

~ SEASON 6, EPISODE 3

MEAT, GAME & ROASTS

ROAST BEEF

Roast beef has long been the pride of English cuisine. As early as the 1600s, foreign visitors to England remarked on the high quality of the meat and the good animal husbandry practices. By the eighteenth century, roast beef had become so synonymous with the English that the French dubbed them *les rosbifs*. About seventy-five years later, with the Napoleonic Wars raging, roast beef in combination with plum pudding became emblematic of English food and English exceptionalism. To serve them at a dinner party was a display of patriotism during wartime. Nineteenth-century Christmas celebrations at Windsor Castle regularly included roast beef. An 1888 photograph shows a full baron of beef displayed alongside such other Christmas icons as boar's head, turkey, game pies, and mince pies.

Of course, a baron of beef (the entire hind quarter of the animal) appeared on the menu only in noble houses. Sirloin and rib roasts were the more common holiday cuts. To celebrate Christmas as was done in the eighteenth century, serve this beef with Christmas Pudding (page 179). If you prefer to dine in the Edwardian era, pair the roast with Yorkshire Pudding (page 121).

SERVES 6

INGREDIENTS

1 beef prime rib, with 3 ribs	2 fresh flat-leaf parsley sprigs
Flaky sea salt	Olive oil, for drizzling
2 carrots, peeled	¼ cup (60 ml) dry white wine
2 ribs celery	1 tablespoon red currant jelly
4 yellow onions	1 tablespoon flour
2 fresh thyme sprigs	3⅓ cups (800 ml) vegetable or beef stock
2 fresh rosemary sprigs	

Remove the beef from the refrigerator about 1 hour before you plan to put it into the oven. Position an oven rack in the lower third of the oven and preheat to 475°F (245°C).

Trim the fat if needed to tidy the edges of the roast. Sprinkle the meat and the fat layer with salt. Check the weight of your roast, as you need to know the weight to calculate the roasting time. For each pound (450 g), figure on 10 minutes for rare, 13–15 minutes for medium-rare, 20 minutes for medium, and 30 minutes for well done.

Roughly chop the carrots, celery, and onions and toss them and the thyme, rosemary, and parsley sprigs into a roasting pan just large enough to hold the roast. Drizzle a little oil over the vegetables and stir to coat them evenly. Place the pan on the stove top over medium heat and cook, stirring occasionally, until the vegetables color slightly and are shiny and showing a golden blush, 5–8 minutes. Place the roast, fat side up, on top of the vegetables and place the pan in the oven.

Roast for 30 minutes, then turn down the oven temperature to 325°F (165°C). Now continue to roast according to the weight of the roast and the desired doneness. To test for doneness, insert an instant-read thermometer into the center of the roast not touching bone; it should register 115°–120°F (46°–49°C) for rare, 120°–125°F (49°–52°C) for medium-rare, 130°–135°F (54°–57°C) for medium, and 150°–155°F (65°–68°C) for well done.

Recipe continues

Remove from the oven, transfer the roast to a warmed plate, tent with aluminum foil, and let rest for 15–20 minutes. Tilt the pan so the fat and pan juices collect in a corner and, using a spoon, skim off as much fat from the surface as possible. Place the pan back on the stove top over medium heat and mash the vegetables with a fork or potato masher. Add the wine, jelly, and flour and stir until the mixture loosens up, about 2 minutes. Pour in the stock, stir well, bring to a simmer, and simmer gently over medium-low heat while the meat rests.

Transfer the roast to a cutting board. Pour any juices that accumulated on the plate during resting into the roasting pan, then bring to a boil over medium heat. Remove from the heat and pour through a fine-mesh sieve into a warmed sauceboat. Carve the roast and serve the pan juices on the side.

. . . dined well on some good ribs of beef roasted and mince-pies . . .

~ *DIARY OF SAMUEL PEPYS,*
PARTIAL ENTRY DECEMBER 25, 1666

DOWNTON TURKEY CHECKLIST

CHOOSING YOUR BIRD

If your budget permits, look for a bird that has been reared naturally, with access to the outdoors and preferably an organic diet. It will have more fat and flavor and is less likely to dry out in the oven. Don't be tempted to choose the largest turkey, as big birds are usually less flavorful and take quite a long time to cook. You may want to try to locate a high-quality turkey farm near you where you can book a bird early on, ensuring you get the best turkey for your Downton-inspired holiday feast. Many independent butchers also offer customers the opportunity to reserve a bird in advance. If possible, avoid purchasing a frozen turkey, which can yield a lesser result. To accommodate the size of your gathering, plan on about 1½ pounds (680 g) of turkey weight for each guest for larger birds. Because smaller birds (under 11 pounds/5 kg) have a lower meat-to-bone ratio, plan on 2 pounds (1 kg) for each guest.

COOK TIMES

If you do purchase a frozen turkey, transfer it from the freezer to the refrigerator to thaw, allowing 24 hours for every 5 pounds (2.3 kg). Then, remove the bird from the refrigerator 2 hours before it goes into the oven (if your Christmas is in summertime and your kitchen is warm, leave the bird at room temperature for less time). Here are cook and rest times that will result in a perfectly roasted turkey.

> 9–11 pounds (4–5 kg): 2½ hours cook time, 1½ hours rest time
> 11–13 pounds (5–6 kg): 2½–3 hours cook time, 1½ hours rest time
> 13–15½ pounds (6–7 kg): 3–3½ hours cook time, 2 hours rest time
> 15½–17½ pounds (7–8 kg): 3½–4 hours cook time, 2 hours rest time
> 17½–20 pounds (8–9 kg): 4–4½ hours cook time, 2 hours rest time

ABOUT THE STUFFING

In *The Cookery Book of Lady Clark of Tillypronie*, a collection of Victorian recipes, Lady Clark suggests stuffing the turkey with whole sausages and whole chestnuts and then making a stuffing for the neck of pounded chestnuts, the liver of the turkey, herbs, and eggs. (She does not mention bread crumbs, which was likely an oversight or perhaps she considered their addition to be understood.) It was also common to serve the turkey *à la chipolata*, or surrounded by small sausages that had been cooked inside the cavity or roasted alongside the bird. But sausage meat was just as often used outside its casing as part of the stuffing mixture.

Nowadays, it is considered unsafe to cook stuffing in the cavity of the bird unless it is removed and then heated to 165°F (74°C) before serving, as the cavity is rarely hot enough to ensure the stuffing is safe to eat. That's why in recent years, with food safety precautions now standard, the stuffing is added only to the neck and the remainder is cooked separately in small balls or baked in a pie or loaf pan. Instead, to infuse the bird as it roasts, the cavity is filled with aromatics and other seasonings, such as onion, lemon, orange, and herbs. The stuffing recipe on page 76 is adapted from the one in Lady Clark's cookery book.

TO SERVE

To serve the turkey on page 76, have ready a warmed large serving platter. Transfer the turkey to a large cutting board. Remove the stuffing from the neck and keep warm. Don kitchen gloves and use your hands to disjoint the legs and wings from the body. Using a sharp boning knife, cut through the bone joints and carve away the legs and wings. Disjoint each thigh from its drumstick and cut through the joints with the knife. Set the thighs, drumsticks, and wings on the serving platter.

For the breasts, first remove the crisp bacon and set aside. Then, to remove the first breast, beginning at the breastbone, place a carving knife right next to it on one side and work your way downward and parallel to the ribcage, working in small strokes if you are not already familiar with carving a turkey. The trick is to stay as close to the ribcage as possible so only a minimal amount of meat remains on the bones. This step takes practice, so you might want to hone your skills throughout the rest of the year on chicken. Repeat on the opposite side to remove the second breast.

Transfer the breasts to a second cutting board, then cut crosswise into slices. Place the breast meat next to the thighs, drumsticks, and wings. Scoop the stuffing onto the platter or transfer it to a warmed bowl for serving. If you are lucky, the crisp bacon will be roughly in the shape of a basket from roasting on top of the bird. Set it on the platter. If the slices have broken apart, dot them around the platter. Either way, diners can take a piece of bacon if they like. Decorate the platter with the fresh herbs.

If you have baked stuffing balls, add them to the serving platter or arrange them on a separate warmed plate. If you have made a stuffing pie, serve it directly from the pan at the table, with a knife on the side, or carefully ease it out of the pan onto a serving plate. If you have used a loaf pan, unmold the stuffing and set it on a rectangular plate or board. Place the turkey platter on the table with the gravy alongside.

ROAST TURKEY

Roasted birds were the headliners of the British meal for centuries, with a few courses building up to them and a few appearing after them. In medieval times, the tables of kings and queens were graced by swans, peacocks, and herons, often roasted and then sewn back into their glorious feathers so they looked alive. Roasted meat was expensive and rare and thus only enjoyed by the privileged. Turkey, introduced from the New World, first appeared in England in the early sixteenth century, but it would be hundreds of years before it would become a Christmas dish.

True roasting requires the radiant heat of an open fire, and in the past, kitchens would have one or more open fireplaces fitted with a spit that was turned by hand or, later, by a roasting jack. Cooking meat in this manner was labor-intensive, as someone was needed to turn the spit by hand if necessary, to baste the meat, and to keep an eye on the fire. In the mid-nineteenth century, the closed range with an oven was introduced. Cooks who knew both open-fire roasting and oven roasting found the former yielded better flavor. But in the end, convenience often won out.

SERVES 8–14, DEPENDING ON THE SIZE OF YOUR TURKEY

INGREDIENTS

1 fresh turkey (see Choosing Your Bird, page 74)

FOR THE STUFFING

6½ oz (185 g) fresh white bread, crusts removed

Whole milk or water, to cover

2 lb (1 kg) pork sausages, casings removed, or loose sausage meat

21 oz (600 g) jarred or vacuum-packed roasted and peeled whole chestnuts (3½–4 cups), crushed with a fork

1 turkey liver or 4 chicken livers, finely chopped

Leaves from 1 large bunch fresh flat-leaf parsley, chopped

10 fresh sage leaves, finely chopped

1 egg, lightly beaten

1 egg yolk, lightly beaten

1 teaspoon black pepper

½ teaspoon salt

Unsalted butter, for frying if cooking balls on the stove top

FOR THE CAVITY

2 yellow onions, halved

1 lemon, halved

1 small bunch fresh rosemary

1 small bunch fresh thyme

1 small bunch fresh flat-leaf parsley

1 small bunch fresh sage

FOR THE PAN

2 yellow onions, chopped

1 large carrot, peeled and chopped

4 cloves garlic, unpeeled and crushed

FOR THE OUTSIDE OF THE BIRD

1 cup (225 g) unsalted butter, at room temperature

Salt and black pepper

6 or 7 fresh sage leaves

6 or 7 fresh bay leaves

7 oz (200 g) bacon slices

FOR THE STUFFING PIE (OPTIONAL)

Flour, for dusting

About 10 oz (285 g) all-butter puff pastry, thawed according to package directions if frozen

2 tablespoons unsalted butter

6 fresh sage leaves

FOR THE GRAVY

4 cups (950 ml) boiling water or chicken stock

2 tablespoons red currant or quince jelly

FOR DECORATION

Fresh herbs, such as rosemary, thyme, and bay leaf

To prepare the turkey for roasting, bring it to room temperature as directed in Cook Times (see page 74). Remove any trussing and pull out the legs a little to allow the hot air to circulate better around them. Check the cavity to see if it contains a bag of giblets. If it does, set aside the liver for the stuffing and reserve the remaining giblets for adding to the roasting pan. To make carving the breasts easier later, remove the wishbone: Lift away the skin covering the neck cavity and, using your fingers, check either side of the inner neck area for the wishbone, which lies just under the flesh. Once you have located one side of the bone, using a small, sharp knife, make a shallow slit in the flesh covering the bone; it must be large enough to allow your fingertips to grasp the bone while you carefully cut along it to the V at the far end. Repeat to free the bone on the other side of the cavity, then gently pull the wishbone from the cavity.

To make the stuffing, put the bread into a bowl and add milk to cover. Let soak until soft, about 30 seconds, then drain, pressing your hand against the bread to force out any excess milk. Transfer the bread to a large bowl, add the sausage, chestnuts, liver, parsley, sage, egg, egg yolk, pepper, and salt, and mix well.

Scoop out 1–1½ cups (250–350 g) of the stuffing, loosely spoon it into the neck cavity, being careful not to pack it too tightly, and then tuck in the skin to hold the stuffing in place. If needed, secure the skin in place with a small metal skewer or a few toothpicks. Shape the rest of the stuffing into small balls the size of a walnut or reserve it for making a stuffing pie. Refrigerate the balls or stuffing.

Put the onions, lemon, rosemary, thyme, parsley, and sage into the body cavity. Select a roasting pan just large enough to hold the turkey and put the onions, carrot, and garlic into the pan along with the giblets, if you have them. Place a roasting rack in the pan.

Now warm the butter between your hands until it becomes very soft and then spread it evenly all over the outside of the bird. Sprinkle the bird all over with salt and pepper, then stick the sage and bay leaves onto the buttered surface, spacing them evenly apart. In the Downton kitchen, we see Daisy laying bacon slices on the turkey at this point, but adding bacon to the raw bird does not give the best result. It is best to add the bacon about 1 hour before the bird is ready, so the bacon is still edible.

Recipe continues

FOOD FOR THOUGHT

In *Kitchen Essays*, published in 1922, Lady Agnes Jekyll describes what she regards as a traditional Christmas of her day.

> Let us, then, keep Christmas with all the time-honoured usages of high festival, and again welcome the turkey, with abundant accompaniments of bread sauce and gravy....Then will there be room also for midget sausages and tiny crisp curls of bacon, for browned or new potatoes (bottled by the prudent), for grilled mushrooms and little balls of stuffing or precious truffles.

To cook the turkey, preheat the oven to 350°F (180°C).

Place a piece of aluminum foil large enough to wrap the entire bird on a work surface. Place a sheet of parchment paper of the same size on top of the foil. Set the bird on the parchment and wrap it in the parchment and foil, covering it completely. This will prevent the bird from coloring too much before it is ready. (In the past, plain paper would have been used for this step.) Place the wrapped bird, breast side up, on the rack in the pan.

Place the pan in the oven and roast the turkey. The timing will depend on its size (see Cook Times on page 74). One hour before the turkey is ready, remove the pan from the oven, unwrap the bird, and cover it with the bacon slices in a neat pattern. Return the pan to the oven and continue to roast the turkey for the remaining time.

The turkey is ready when an instant-read thermometer inserted into the thickest part of the breast and the innermost part of the thigh without touching bone registers 150°F (65°C). In the absence of a thermometer, pierce the thickest part of the thigh with a knife; if the juices run clear, the turkey is done.

Remove the pan from the oven and carefully tip the turkey so the juices in the cavity flow into the pan. Then remove and discard the onions, lemon, and herbs from the cavity and transfer the bird to a warmed plate. Place a piece of foil large enough to cover the turkey on a work surface, top with a second piece of foil of the same size, and then with a piece of parchment the same size as the foil. Cover the bird with the stacked layers, parchment side down. Lay a kitchen towel over the top and let rest for 1½–2 hours, depending on the size of your turkey.

While the turkey is resting, cook the stuffing and make the gravy. To fry the stuffing balls, melt 1–2 tablespoons butter in a large frying pan over medium heat. Add the balls and cook, turning as needed, until browned on all sides and cooked through, 25–30 minutes. Set aside and keep warm.

If you decide to make the stuffing pie instead of the balls, this is when it should be baked. Position a rack in the lower third of the oven and preheat the oven 350°F (180°C). Have ready a pie pan

RECIPE NOTE

Pan Potatoes (page 127) or roast potatoes usually accompany the turkey, and Bread Sauce (page 150) is often served along with gravy.

measuring 8½–9½ inches (21.5–24-cm) in diameter. On a lightly floured work surface, roll out the pastry about 3 inches (7.5 cm) larger than the pan diameter. Transfer the pastry to the pan, pressing it gently onto the bottom and up the sides. Pierce the bottom all over with a fork, then trim the overhang and crimp the edge attractively. Drop dollops of the stuffing onto the pastry, then spread the stuffing gently and evenly in the pan. Cut the butter into bits and dot the stuffing, then top the stuffing with the sage leaves. If you opt to omit the pastry, spoon the stuffing into a 9 x 5-inch (23 x 13-cm) loaf pan, dot the surface with the butter, and top with the sage leaves. Bake the pastry-lined stuffing pie in the lower third of the oven for about 15 minutes, then move the pan to the center rack and bake until the pastry is puffed and golden brown, about 15 minutes longer. If using a loaf pan, bake on the center rack until an instant-read thermometer inserted into the center of the loaf registers 165°F (74°C), about 1 hour.

To prepare the gravy, tilt the roasting pan slightly so the fat and pan juices collect in one corner and, using a spoon, skim off most of the fat from the surface of the juices (you can discard the fat or reserve it for making roast potatoes or for using it in place of butter or olive oil for Pan Potatoes on page 127). Place the pan on the stove top over medium heat and crush the vegetables with a fork or a potato masher. If you added the giblets, they can stay in the pan too, though they won't be crushed, which is fine. Pour in the boiling water, add the jelly, and heat, stirring, until the gravy is reduced to your liking. Remove from the heat and strain through a fine-mesh sieve into a saucepan, discarding the solids. Reheat the gravy just before serving and transfer to a warmed sauceboat.

To serve the turkey, first uncover it and carry it into the dining room to show your guests. Then return to the kitchen to carve it following the instructions on page 75.

DOWNTON NOTE

For noble houses, roast beef was still the centerpiece of the Christmas table, with game and turkey playing supporting roles. But at Downton, possibly because of the influence of American-born Lady Grantham, the turkey is more prominently featured than other meats on the holiday menu. We see evidence of this in the Christmas episode in season 5, with Daisy busy preparing the Christmas turkey, which occupies the center of the kitchen table. She carefully drapes the gigantic raw beast with crisscrossed slices of bacon, while tucking bay leaves under the slices. Next to the bird is a large bowl of stuffing from which she has already made little balls to serve alongside the carved turkey at the table.

ROAST GOOSE

This recipe for goose comes from *The Forme of Cury*, a scroll of recipes that dates to around 1390. It is the earliest collection of recipes in the English language, and the "chief master cooks" of Richard II are credited as its authors. Goose was already a Christmas bird in the fourteenth century, so we can assume this dish might well have appeared as part of the king's holiday feast.

The goose is stuffed with herbs, quinces, pears, and grapes, and the rich dark meat pairs particularly well with the sourness of the quinces. To accompany the roast goose, you first prepare a galyntyne sauce, a classic medieval accompaniment to roast meats made from wine, vinegar, and spices and thickened with bread, which you then mix with the stuffing to make a fruit sauce. Among the spices in the galyntyne sauce is galangal, a tropical rhizome related to ginger and most commonly used today in Asian recipes. Although fresh galangal is difficult to find outside of Southeast and South Asia, dried galangal, which is carried in Asian shops and online, can be used for this recipe.

SERVES 6–8

INGREDIENTS

I goose, 9–II lb (4–5 kg)

FOR THE STUFFING

2 quinces, peeled, cored, and chopped

2 pears, peeled, cored, and chopped

⅔ cup (100 g) seedless grapes, any kind

I clove garlic

2 fresh flat-leaf parsley sprigs

2 fresh hyssop or oregano sprigs

2 fresh savory sprigs

I fresh sage sprig

FOR THE GALYNTYNE SAUCE

½ cup (120 ml) red wine, red port, or Madeira, plus more if needed for thinning

3 tablespoons red wine vinegar or cider vinegar

½ cup (50 g) dried bread crumbs

I teaspoon ground dried galangal

¼ teaspoon ground cinnamon

¼ teaspoon ground ginger

Salt

To prepare the goose for roasting, remove it from the refrigerator I hour before it will go into the oven. (If your Christmas is in summertime and your kitchen is warm, leave the bird at room temperature for less time.) Remove any trussing and pull out the legs a little to allow the hot air to circulate better around them. There are two large lobes of fat on either side of the opening of the body cavity that you can either remove now and render down for use in other recipes or leave in place to render as the goose roasts.

To make carving the breasts easier later, remove the wishbone: Lift away the skin covering the neck cavity and, using your fingers, check either side of the inner neck area for the wishbone, which lies just under the flesh. Once you have located one side of the bone, using a small, sharp knife, make a shallow slit in the flesh covering the bone; it must be large enough to allow your fingertips to grasp the bone while you carefully cut along it to the V at the far end. Repeat to free the bone on the other side of the cavity, then gently pull the wishbone from the cavity.

To make the stuffing, in a bowl, combine the quinces, pears, grapes, and garlic. Bruise all the herb sprigs by rubbing them in your hands, add them to the bowl, and mix well. Using a large spoon or your hand, transfer the stuffing to the cavity of the goose. Then with a trussing needle and kitchen string, sew the cavity closed. Alternatively, skewer closed with metal trussing skewers, then lace the skewers with kitchen string.

Preheat the oven to 400°F (200°C).

Select a roasting pan just large enough to accommodate the goose and place a roasting rack in it. A goose has a layer of fat under the skin that will melt and drip from the bird during roasting, so the rack ensures that the melting fat will collect in the pan with the drippings. (After the goose is roasted, you can collect the fat, strain it, and use it in other recipes, such as the Pan Potatoes on page 127, where it can replace the butter or oil, or for roast potatoes.) Set the goose, breast side up, on the rack.

Roast the goose for 3½ hours, turning down the oven temperature to 350°F (180°C) after the first 10 minutes. If the breast is browning too quickly and the goose still has a while to cook, make a hood for the breast by layering a piece of aluminum foil large enough to cover the breast with a piece of parchment paper of equal size, then place them, parchment side down, over the breast. Fold the entire edge of the foil under the pan to keep the hood in place. If you are planning to capture the melting goose fat to use for cooking potatoes, scoop out some of the fat with a ladle about halfway through the roasting time. After 3½ hours, an instant-read thermometer inserted into the thickest part of the breast and the innermost part of the thigh without touching bone should register 165°F (74°C).

Although you may want to show your guests your beautiful whole roasted Christmas goose just before you carve it, it is better to remove the legs and roast them longer before carving. If you don't, the breast meat will be overcooked by the time the legs are perfectly cooked. So here's what you do: Remove the goose from the oven and present it to your guests. After a few oohs and aahs, tell everyone the goose will be served in about 30 minutes. In reality, it will be a little longer, but no one will notice. Return the goose to the kitchen, carve off the legs, wrap the whole bird in foil, cover it with a kitchen towel, and place it on a warmed sheet pan.

Tilt the roasting pan slightly so the fat and drippings collect in a corner; the drippings will settle to the bottom and the fat will rise

Recipe continues

RECIPE NOTE

Leftover roast goose makes a delicious cold salad or a luxurious Boxing Day sandwich. If you've used all the sauce, serve with a quince compote. Rinse 4 quinces well, put them into a saucepan, add water to cover generously, and bring to a boil. Adjust the heat to maintain a steady slow boil and cook until a metal skewer inserted into a quince meets little resistance, about 1 hour. Drain, let cool until they can be handled, and then peel, quarter, core, and cut into smaller pieces. Return the pieces to the pan, add 1¼ cups (300 ml) dry red wine, juice of 2 lemons, 1 cinnamon stick, 3 whole cloves, and 1 small bay leaf and bring to a simmer over medium heat. Simmer gently until the quince pieces are soft but not falling apart. Remove from the heat, scoop out the spices and bay leaf, and serve warm or cold.

ROBERT: *The English have strong principles, except when it comes to the chance of good shooting or eating well.*

~ SEASON 5, EPISODE 9

to the top. Spoon off the fat from the surface of the drippings and strain it through a fine-mesh sieve into a heatproof glass jar. Let the fat cool and solidify, then refrigerate and use in other recipes. (Or transfer the fat to a plastic container or an ice-cube tray, let cool and solidify, then freeze.) Spoon ⅓ cup (80 ml) of the drippings into a saucepan and set aside for the sauce. Place the legs on the roasting rack, pop the pan back into the oven, and roast the legs until the meat falls easily from the bone, about 30 minutes. (If your party is smaller than eight, you can save the legs as leftovers and finish roasting them the next day.)

When the legs are ready, remove from the oven and turn up the oven temperature to 400°F (200°C). Unwrap the goose, remove the trussing from the cavity, and scoop the stuffing into a large, heavy sauceapn, discarding the herb sprigs. Re-cover the goose.

To make the galyntyne sauce, add the wine, vinegar, bread crumbs, galangal, cinnamon, and ginger to the drippings in the saucepan and place over medium heat. Bring to a simmer and simmer, stirring frequently, until the mixture is smooth and thickened, 5–8 minutes. Pour it into the saucepan holding the stuffing, place the pan over medium heat, and bring to a boil, stirring to prevent scorching. Continue to boil, stirring often, until the mixture is the consistency of a thick, pourable applesauce, 10–12 minutes. If it is too thick, add more wine to achieve a thick pouring consistency. Season with salt. Keep warm.

To carve the goose, unwrap it and place on a cutting board. Have a large warmed serving plate ready. To remove the wings, disjoint a wing with your hands, then, using a sharp boning knife, cut through the joint to free the wing. Repeat with the other wing.

To remove the first breast, beginning at the breastbone, place a carving knife right next to it on one side and work your way downward and parallel to the ribcage, staying as close to the ribcage as possible so only minimal meat remains on the bones. Set the breast aside and remove the second breast the same way.

If by now the meat feels like it has lost too much heat, place the whole breasts and the legs on an ovenproof serving tray and pop them back into the oven for about 10 minutes. They should be just warmed through. This step also has the advantage of heating the serving tray. See Recipe Note for serving instructions.

RECIPE NOTE

To serve the goose, cut the breasts into slices and arrange them on the serving tray or a warmed platter. Pull the meat off the leg bones and place it around the breast slices. Pour the sauce into a warmed sauceboat. If there is space on the serving tray or platter, put the sauceboat on it. If not, set the sauceboat alongside the goose on the table.

MATTHEW: *Are you a hunting family?*

MARY: *Families like ours are always hunting families.*

~ SEASON 1, EPISODE 2

DUCK WITH ORANGE, LEMON, AND OLIVES

This recipe comes from Georgina Ward, Countess of Dudley, a young Scottish noblewoman who decided to note down her simple—as she called them—recipes with clear instructions. Published in 1909, *The Dudley Book of Cookery and Household Recipes* proved popular, and a second volume followed a few years later. Her recipes were inspired by cuisines all over Europe, and at the same time, she included many very English recipes that she made sound French, such as her Duck à la Langham, from which this recipe is adapted. She calls for a fat Rouen or Aylesbury duck, both popular English breeds at the time. Giving the reader these two choices was thoughtful and practical, as the Aylesbury duck was sold primarily in spring and summer and the Rouen in winter.

SERVES 6

INGREDIENTS

I duck, about 5 lb (2.3 kg)

2 carrots, peeled

2 ribs celery

2 yellow onions

2 fresh flat-leaf parsley sprigs

2 fresh thyme sprigs

I bay leaf

I lemon, halved

7 tablespoons (100 g) unsalted butter, melted (preferably clarified butter; see Recipe Note on page 86)

Flaky sea salt

FOR THE SAUCE

2½ cups (600 ml) curaçao

1¼ cups (300 ml) red port

Juice of I lemon

Juice of I orange

Cornstarch, if needed for thickening

FOR THE GARNISH

1½ cups (225 g) raisins

Red port, to cover

10 small oranges

3 lemons

6½ tablespoons (100 ml) Madeira, plus more if needed

I lb (450 g) pitted green olives

Fresh parsley (optional)

Remove the duck from the refrigerator about I hour before it will go into the oven (if your Christmas is in summertime and your kitchen is warm, leave the bird at room temperature for less time). Preheat the oven to 350°F (180°C).

Roughly chop the carrots, celery, and onions and toss them along with the parsley, thyme, and bay leaf into a roasting pan just large enough to hold the duck. Place the duck, breast side up, on the vegetables and slip the lemon halves into the cavity. Pour the butter evenly over the duck, then sprinkle the duck with salt.

Roast the duck until golden brown, about I½ hours. Remove the pan from the oven. Transfer the duck to a sheet pan. Carefully tilt the roasting pan so the fat and drippings collect in a corner and spoon off the fat from the surface of the drippings. (If you like frying potatoes and other vegetables in duck fat, transfer the fat to a heatproof container, pouring it through a fine-mesh sieve, then let cool and refrigerate.) Return the duck to the roasting pan.

Recipe continues

To make the sauce, pour the curaçao, port, and lemon and orange juices into the roasting pan.

Return the pan to the oven for about 30 minutes. Each duck is different, so your duck could take a bit longer or a bit less time to finish cooking. Begin checking for doneness after about 20 minutes. Roast duck is generally served pink, so an instant-read thermometer inserted into the leg without touching bone should register 125°F (52°C). Or if you prefer it cooked through, roast until it registers 160°F (71°C).

While the duck roasts, begin making the garnish. In a small saucepan, combine the raisins with port to cover, bring to a gentle simmer over medium-low heat, and simmer for 15 minutes, then remove from the heat and set aside. Meanwhile, using a small, sharp knife, cut a thin slice off the top and bottom of an orange. Stand the orange upright and, following the contour of the fruit, slice downward to remove the peel and pith, rotating the orange after each slice. Set the peel aside and quarter the orange. Peel and quarter 7 more oranges and 2 of the lemons the same way. Toss the citrus quarters into a saucepan and add the Madeira, adding more if needed to cover. Bring to a gentle simmer over medium-low heat and simmer for 5 minutes. Remove from the heat and set aside.

Scrape off the white pith from the peels of 4 of the oranges and the 2 lemons (discard the remaining peels), then cut the peels lengthwise into narrow strips. In a saucepan, combine the peel strips with water to cover, bring to a boil over medium-high heat, and cook until tender, about 10 minutes. Remove from the heat, drain, and reserve.

When the duck is ready, transfer it to a warmed plate and tent with aluminum foil to keep warm. To finish the sauce, pour the contents of the roasting pan into a fine-mesh sieve placed over a saucepan and discard the solids.

Bring the liquid in the saucepan to a simmer over medium-high heat. Drain the raisins into a sieve over the saucepan and set the raisins aside. Then drain the citrus quarters the same way and set

RECIPE NOTE

Clarified butter has a wonderful nutty flavor and high smoke point, making it a good choice for this duck recipe (store-bought ghee is an easy substitute). For ease, it is best to clarify at least 1 cup (225 g) butter; any leftover clarified butter will keep in an airtight container in the refrigerator for up to 2 months. Slowly melt the butter in a small saucepan over low heat. When it has fully melted, using a spoon, skim off as much foam from the surface as possible. Remove the pan from the heat and let sit for 5 minutes. The milk solids will sink to the bottom of the pan. Carefully pour off the clear, golden liquid through a fine-mesh sieve placed over a bowl. Discard the solids in the sieve.

the citrus aside with the raisins. Simmer until the liquid reduces and thickens to a good sauce consistency. If it is not thickening sufficiently, put about 1 tablespoon cornstarch into a small bowl, add a few spoonfuls of the hot liquid, and stir to dissolve the cornstarch, then whisk the slurry into the simmering sauce.

To serve, place the whole duck in the center of a warmed serving platter and arrange the reserved citrus quarters, raisins, and citrus strips and the olives attractively around the bird. Carry the platter to the dining table to show your guests, then immediately return to the kitchen with it.

To carve the duck, transfer it to a cutting board. To remove a leg, cut between the breast and the leg, running your knife around the back of the thigh. Be careful not to miss the "oyster," the small, round, particularly delicious piece of meat near the backbone. Remove the other leg the same way. Cut down between the thigh and drumstick of each leg and set all the pieces aside. To remove the first breast, beginning at the breastbone, place a carving knife right next to it on one side and work your way downward and parallel to the ribcage, staying as close to the ribcage as possible so only minimal meat remains on the bones. Remove the second breast the same way. The breasts can be sliced or halved for serving. To remove each wing, cut through the joint between the wing and the ribcage.

Arrange all the duck pieces on the platter and attractively distribute the citrus quarters, raisins, citrus strips, and olives in among the pieces. Pour some of the sauce around the duck and then pour the remainder into a warmed sauceboat to serve alongside. Cut the remaining 2 oranges and 1 lemon into wedges and set them around the platter, then garnish with parsley, if using, and serve.

FOOD FOR THOUGHT

The white-feathered Aylesbury duck has been bred in the Buckinghamshire town of Aylesbury since the nineteenth century. Historically, there were two types of producers: breeders who reared their pedigree stock, and duckers who bought fertilized eggs from the breeders to hatch themselves. Many of the duckers lived in an area of the town known as Duck End, and they often raised the ducklings in their homes. It was usually a secondary income for the family, and newly hatched ducklings would be cared for by the women of the household until they reached eight weeks, when they were slaughtered. Some cottages had ducks in every room, all carefully contained in rows of hay-lined wooden boxes. In *Mrs Beeton's Book of Household Management*, the author notes that the Aylesbury duck was reared "not on plains and commons" but in cottages.

When the railway came to Aylesbury in 1839, duck producers could get their product to London more quickly, and Aylesbury ducks became more affordable. By the beginning of the twentieth century, the Aylesbury duck was in decline, with a hardier breed, the Pekin, taking over. However, in 1908, just a year before Lady Dudley published her first book, the Aylesbury duck enjoyed renewed interest, thanks to Beatrix Potter's character Jemima Puddle-Duck. But World War I and then World War II continued the previous weakening of the market, eventually wiping out nearly all of the producers. By 1966, no Aylesbury duck breeders remained.

But this story has a happy ending. By 2015, there were Aylesbury ducks again, this time in Chesham, not far from Aylesbury. They are being reared by Richard Waller, who comes from a family of Aylesbury duck producers that dates back to circa 1775. Although a common breed in the nineteenth century, the Aylesbury duck is now a heritage breed.

ROAST VENISON

Venison is lean, so you need to add fat. The original recipe, which appears in Dorothy Allhusen's *A Book of Scents and Dishes*, calls for larding the meat well. This technique was done by using a larding needle to weave long, narrow strips of fat throughout the roast. Because not everyone has such a nifty tool today, the larding has been replaced here with bacon slices, which are laid over the meat. While larding would still have been common in Mrs. Patmore's time, we see Daisy using the more modern bacon method for the Christmas turkey in season 5. It is best to sear the venison before adding the bacon to ensure the exterior of the meat has a nice, rich look when it is served. Pan Potatoes (page 127) or roast potatoes are an excellent accompaniment.

SERVES 6

INGREDIENTS

1 rolled venison roast (from the leg), about 3 lb (1.4 kg)

FOR THE MARINADE

Buttermilk, to cover

3 small yellow onions, each studded with 3 whole cloves

10 black peppercorns

4 fresh or dried bay leaves

6 fresh or dried thyme sprigs

6 fresh or dried rosemary sprigs

6 fresh flat-leaf parsley sprigs

2 tablespoons unsalted butter, plus more if needed

10 bacon slices

2 tablespoons red currant jelly

Salt and black pepper

Prune Sauce (page 156) or cranberry compote, for serving

Put the roast in a deep bowl or other deep container. To make the marinade, add enough buttermilk to the bowl to cover the venison. Add the onions, peppercorns, bay leaves, and thyme, rosemary, and parsley sprigs, pushing them down into the buttermilk. Cover the bowl and refrigerate for at least 12 hours or up to 24 hours. (In the Downton era, in wintertime, the venison would have been left to marinate in a cold room.) The older the animal from which the roast was taken, the longer the meat should marinate to tenderize it.

On the day of serving, remove the bowl from the refrigerator 2 hours before you plan to put the roast into the oven. Preheat the oven to 425°F (220°C).

Remove the meat from the marinade and reserve the marinade to use for basting the roast. Pat the meat dry with paper towels.

Select a roasting pan just large enough to hold the roast, set it on the stove top over medium-low heat, and add the butter. When the butter melts, increase the heat to medium, add the roast, and brown on all sides, turning as needed and adding more butter if needed. Transfer the roast to a plate, then remove the pan from the stove top.

Place a roasting rack in the roasting pan and set the roast on the rack. Drape the bacon slices over the roast, covering it completely. Place the pan in the oven and roast the venison for 20 minutes. Baste the venison with 2 tablespoons of the marinade, then reduce the oven temperature to 325°F (165°C) and continue to roast for about 24 minutes for rare or about

30 minutes for medium-rare. The roast is ready when an instant-read thermometer inserted into the center of the roast registers 130°–135°F (54°–57°C) for rare or 135°–140°F (57°–60°C) for medium-rare. It is best not to serve venison well done because the meat will be dry from the long cooking.

Remove the pan from the oven and transfer the roast to a warmed plate. Tent with aluminum foil and let rest for 20 minutes.

While the roast rests, place the roasting pan over medium heat on the stove top, stir in the jelly, bring to a simmer, and simmer until the pan juices have reduced and thickened to a nice gravy consistency, about 5 minutes. Add any juices that have accumulated on the plate on which the roast is resting. Remove from the heat, season with salt and pepper, and strain through a fine-mesh sieve into a warmed sauceboat.

Snip the strings on the roast, cut into slices, and serve warm, accompanied with the gravy and the Prune Sauce.

MARY: *Well done, Papa. Your reward will be to join the ladies' lunch.*

ROBERT: *An added bonus. I hope it's venison.*

ROSE: *Quite right. We ought to eat what we kill.*

~ SEASON 3, EPISODE 9

BOXING DAY

Boxing Day is a secular holiday celebrated in England and other Commonwealth countries on the day after Christmas. It has been a bank holiday in England since 1871, and although now it's a big day for sports, with national football and rugby matches filling stadiums and horse-racing tracks crowded with punters, the day has nothing to do with the sport of boxing and everything to do with boxes.

In medieval times, December 26 was a day of charity. At Christmastime, alms boxes were placed in churches to collect money for the poor. On the day after Christmas, the feast day of Saint Stephen, the boxes were opened and their contents distributed to the needy.

By the eighteenth century, the alms boxes of the Middle Ages had given way to Christmas boxes, as this extract from *Round about Our Coal-fire, or, Christmas Entertainments*, published circa 1740, describes: "Then for your Christmas Box. / Sweet Plumb-cakes and money, / Delicate Holland Smocks, / Kisses Sweet as Honey." A little over two decades later, famed diarist Samuel Pepys writes of putting something in "the boys' box" and of giving money to a local tradesman.

A century later, William Henry Husk, in his 1868 *Songs of the Nativity*, writes that the custom of giving Christmas boxes was "fast approaching to extinction. . . . Formerly nearly every person who had, or was supposed to have, rendered services to another during the year, looked for a gratuity at Christmas, and in many cases it was regarded almost as a right." He was recalling a time when everyone from chimney sweeps, clerics, and the lamplighter to bank clerks, the shoemaker, and the neighborhood bobby would have expected at least a few pennies toward their Christmas box. Servants who worked in the houses of the upper class were usually given not only small gifts but also leftovers from the Christmas feast, which they would box up to take home to share with their families.

Although the moneyed classes in the period when Downton was set continued to maintain some aspects of the Christmas box custom, they also saw Boxing Day as yet another holiday on which to enjoy themselves. For the Crawleys and for many families with grand estates, hosting a hunt on Boxing Day was as traditional as the Christmas pudding. At the end of the hunt, an elaborate luncheon would be served in the field under a marquee. Any guests who did not ride would travel to the site to join the hunting party for a menu typically made up of easy-to-transport foods that could be eaten cold, with savory pies a great favorite (see pages 106–119).

MUTTON CHOPS WITH CRISPY HERB CRUST

Mutton chops were popular in Victorian and Edwardian times. They have more hard marbled fat than lamb chops because they come from older sheep. The age of the animal also means the chops need to cook longer, but the extra fat keeps the meat moist. Lamb, in contrast, is usually served pink, which is difficult to do when making this recipe, as the chops are cooked twice, on a griddle and under a broiler.

If your regular butcher counter doesn't sell mutton, it's worth the effort to seek out small independent butchers who cater to cooks preparing Middle Eastern, African, or South Asian cuisine. Or, if you live in or near a rural area, you might be able to find mutton through a local farmer. If all you can buy is lamb, ask your butcher to cut two-bone chops instead of the usual one bone so the rib eye is thicker.

SERVES 4

INGREDIENTS

FOR THE TOPPING

¼ lb (115 g) ground mutton or lamb

1 egg, lightly beaten

⅓ cup (40 g) dried bread crumbs, or ⅔ cup (40 g) panko (Japanese bread crumbs), plus more for sprinkling

⅓ cup (40 g) grated Parmesan cheese, plus more for sprinkling

2 tablespoons finely chopped fresh flat-leaf parsley

Pinch of salt

Pinch of black pepper

12 mutton or double-thick lamb rib chops (see headnote), about 7 oz (200 g) each

Unsalted butter or olive oil, for frying

Unsalted butter, cut into ¼-inch (6-mm) cubes, for topping the meat

Preheat the broiler, positioning a rack about 4½ inches (11.5 cm) from the heat source. Line a large sheet pan with parchment paper.

To make the topping, in a bowl, combine the mutton, egg, bread crumbs, Parmesan, parsley, salt, and pepper and mix well. Divide the mixture into 12 equal portions and shape each portion into a ball.

Place a stove-top griddle or a frying pan over high heat. When the griddle is hot, stand the chops on their fat side to brown the fat. If you are using lamb, the fat layer may not be very thick, and you will need to fry it only briefly. Then, working in batches, add a little butter and fry the chops on both sides until browned but not cooked through, about 8 minutes on each side. As the chops are ready, transfer them to the prepared sheet pan.

When all the chops are browned and on the pan, place a topping ball on the eye of each chop and press down on it so it becomes a little mound. Sprinkle a little Parmesan followed by some bread crumbs over each mound, then dot each chop with 3 butter cubes.

Slide the pan under the broiler and broil until the topping on each chop is golden brown, 10–15 minutes. Serve warm.

STUFFED LEG OF MUTTON

For centuries, mutton was a staple meat of the British table, served for everyday fare, for celebratory feasts, and, of course, for Christmas. In *Mrs Beeton's Book of Household Management*, the author praises the role of mutton in the British kitchen: "Of all wild or domesticated animals, the sheep is, without exception, the most useful to man as a food and the most necessary to his health and comfort. Mutton is, undoubtedly, the meat most generally used in families." It would have regularly been on the menu at Downton because Yorkshire, where the estate is located, was an important wool-producing area, and mutton traditionally came from retired wool sheep, who would have grazed on the fresh grass, flowers, and herbs of the local landscape their entire lives.

There really is no meat quite like mutton, which has a complex, fragrant flavor and robust texture because the sheep are at least two years old when they are slaughtered. But raising sheep for wool is no longer as prevalent in Britain, and mutton has become rare, as raising lamb for the market yields a far quicker return. This dish can be made with lamb, but if you can find mutton, the result will be more flavorsome.

SERVES 6

INGREDIENTS

I boneless half leg of mutton, about 3½ lb (1.6 kg)

FOR THE FORCEMEAT

I tablespoon unsalted butter

5 oz (140 g) white mushrooms, brushed clean and cut into ¼-inch (6-mm) cubes

I shallot, minced

Pinch of ground nutmeg

Pinch of ground mace

Black pepper or cayenne pepper

I tablespoon chopped fresh flat-leaf parsley

2 teaspoons chopped fresh thyme or marjoram

Grated zest of ½ lemon

¼ cup (25 g) dried bread crumbs

2 teaspoons unsalted butter, at room temperature

I egg yolk, lightly beaten

2 carrots, peeled

2 ribs celery

4 yellow onions

Olive oil, for drizzling

¼ cup (60 ml) dry red wine

I tablespoon red currant jelly

Salt and black pepper

Fresh rosemary sprigs, for garnish (optional)

Remove the mutton from the refrigerator about I hour before you plan to stuff it.

To make the forcemeat, in a large frying pan, melt the butter over medium heat. Toss in the mushrooms and shallot and leave for a minute or so. Then start stirring the mushrooms and cook until they have taken on color and have reduced by half in volume, about 4 minutes. Season with the nutmeg and mace and with pepper to taste. Transfer the mushrooms to a bowl and let cool.

Fold the parsley, thyme, lemon zest, and bread crumbs into the cooled mushrooms. Pop in the butter and, using clean hands or a large wooden spoon, mix everything together well. Then add the egg yolk and continue to mix until fully blended.

Preheat the oven to 400°F (200°C).

Put the mutton, skin side down, on a large cutting board and open it out flat. If some areas are thicker than others, slash them with a knife so the meat is as even as possible. Scoop the forcemeat lengthwise along the center of the leg. Fold the short ends inward, then roll up the meat lengthwise and tie securely with kitchen string at 2-inch (5-cm) intervals.

Recipe continues

Roughly chop the carrots, celery, and onions and toss them into a roasting pan just large enough to hold the stuffed leg. Drizzle the vegetables with oil and stir to coat evenly. Place the pan on the stove top over medium heat and cook, stirring occasionally, until the vegetables color slightly and are shiny and showing a golden blush, about 5 minutes. Place the stuffed leg on top of the vegetables and place the pan in the oven.

Roast the leg until it is browned, 20–30 minutes. Reduce the oven temperaure to 375°F (190°C) and continue to roast until an instant-read thermometer inserted into the center of the roast registers 145°F (63°C) for medium-rare, about 1 hour longer, or until done to your liking. (The cooking method and time for mutton and lamb will be similar.)

Remove the pan from the oven, transfer the mutton to a warm plate, tent with aluminum foil, and let rest for at least 15 minutes while you make the gravy. Tilt the pan so the fat and juices collect in a corner and spoon off the fat. Place the pan on the stove top over medium heat, bring to a simmer, and reduce the liquid slightly. Add the wine and jelly, stir to mix, and strain through a fine-mesh sieve into a small saucepan. Bring to a simmer over medium heat and reduce to a gravy consistency, about 15 minutes. Season with salt and pepper.

To serve, snip the strings on the mutton and cut into slices about ¾ inch (2 cm) thick. Transfer to a warmed platter and garnish with rosemary, if using. Pour the gravy into a warmed sauceboat and offer on the side.

VIOLET: *Oh my dear, in my time, I wore the crinoline, the bustle and the leg-of-mutton sleeve. I am not in a strong position to criticise.*

~ SEASON 3, EPISODE 9

TOURNEDOS VICTORIA

In her highly regarded *A Book of Scents and Dishes*, published in the 1920s, Dorothy Allhusen credits Monsieur Herbodean of London's Ritz Hotel with this recipe and three others. Dishes with the names Victoria and Albert were incredibly popular well into the twentieth century, and even today continue to appeal to the imagination of many English cooks. This dish is traditionally served with stuffed tomatoes, such as the Tomatoes à la Bruxelles on page 128.

SERVES 4

INGREDIENTS

2 large tomatoes, about 7 oz (200 g) each

4 veal or beef tournedos (cut from the smaller end of the tenderloin), each 5½–7 oz (155–200 g) and about ¾ inch (2 cm) thick

Salt and black pepper

1 tablespoon plus 1 teaspoon unsalted butter

1 small shallot, finely minced

6 oz (170 g) white mushrooms, brushed clean and sliced

½ cup (120 ml) dry white wine

3 tablespoons chopped fresh tarragon

1 tablespoon chopped fresh flat-leaf parsley

Have ready a large bowl of ice-cold water. Bring a saucepan of water to a boil over high heat. Lightly score an X on the blossom end of each tomato; this will help speed peeling. Carefully lower the tomatoes into the boiling water and boil for about 15 seconds (start counting when the water begins to bubble again). You should see the skin begin to wrinkle slightly. Using a slotted spoon, transfer the tomatoes to the ice-cold water. As soon as the tomatoes are cool, peel off their skin and dry them. Cut the tomatoes crosswise into slices about ½ inch (12 cm) thick.

Have ready a sheet of aluminum foil or 2 large warmed plates for holding the meat. Prepare the remaining vegetables and the herbs.

Season the tournedos all over with salt. In a large frying pan, melt 1 tablespoon of the butter over medium heat. When the butter is hot, place the tournedos in the pan and fry, turning once and seasoning the cooked sides with pepper, until cooked to desired doneness, about 7 minutes on each side for medium-rare. Transfer the tournedos to the foil and wrap loosely or put on a warmed plate and invert the second plate on top.

Return the pan to medium heat and melt the remaining 1 teaspoon butter. Add the shallot and mushrooms and cook, stirring, until the mushrooms are browned, about 4 minutes. Add the tomatoes and cook, turning, until they begin to caramelize, about 5 minutes. Pour in the wine and deglaze the pan, stirring to dislodge any browned bits from the pan bottom, then simmer until the wine reduces by about two-thirds. Stir in the tarragon and parsley.

Arrange the vegetables on an oval serving platter, place the tournedos on top, and serve.

JUGGED HARE WITH PRUNES AND RAISINS

Traditionally, jugged cooking is the cooking of a whole hare or other small animal in a tightly covered earthenware jug. Today, an enameled cast-iron pot usually takes the place of the jug, though if you have a large ovenproof jug, you can stand it in a pot of simmering water in the oven.

The dish is also linked to one of the most inaccurately cited references in culinary history: "First, catch your hare." According to legend, this straightforward instruction comes from *The Art of Cookery Made Plain and Easy* by London-born Hannah Glasse, which was first published in the 1740s and remained a best-seller for more than a century. However, the actual direction was, "Take your Hare when it is cas'd . . . ," which means to start with a skinned animal (the now-archaic "to case" means "to skin an animal").

Hare remains a popular game meat in England, and its blood is especially prized for the making of the sauce or gravy to accompany it. If you are able to acquire the blood along with the hare, stir it into the sauce just before returning the hare to the pot to warm for serving.

SERVES 4–6

INGREDIENTS

I whole hare, about 3 lb (1.4 kg), cut into 6 serving pieces, or about 2 lb (1 kg) hare saddles (about 6 fillets)

Flour, for dusting

I tablespoon unsalted butter

2 yellow onions, chopped

¼ lb (115 g) prunes, pitted (about ⅔ cup)

⅓ cup (55 g) dark or golden raisins

1¼ cups (300 ml) game or beef stock

½ teaspoon salt

Black pepper

Pinch of sugar

I tablespoon red currant jelly

⅔ cup (160 ml) dry red wine

Preheat the oven to 325°F (165°C).

Dust the hare pieces with flour, coating evenly and tapping off the excess. In a large, heavy pot, melt the butter over medium heat. When the butter bubbles, add the hare pieces, in batches to avoid crowding, and cook, turning as needed, until nicely browned on all sides, 5–8 minutes. As each batch is ready, transfer it to a plate.

When all the pieces are browned, return them to the pot and toss in the onions, prunes, and raisins. Pour in the stock and add the salt, a generous turning of the pepper mill, and the sugar. Bring to a simmer over medium heat, cover, transfer the pot to the oven, and braise the hare for 1½ hours. The meat should be tender when pierced with a fork but not falling apart.

Remove the pot from the oven, transfer the meat to a warmed plate, and cover with aluminum foil to keep warm. Return the pot to the stove top over medium heat. Stir the jelly into the cooking liquid in the pot, then pour in the wine, bring to a simmer, and simmer until the sauce thickens, about 5 minutes.

Return the meat to the pot to rewarm in the sauce, then transfer to warmed individual plates, placing I piece or fillet on each plate. Spoon enough of the sauce over the meat so it is moistened and shiny. Transfer the remaining sauce to a small warmed tureen and ladle it over the meat at the table, making sure everyone gets some prunes and raisins.

COQ AU VIN

Coq au vin translates to "rooster in wine," and although today in France and Belgium the dish is still on rare occasions made with a rooster, Mrs. Patmore—and modern cooks—would have preferred a plump hen, which needs much less cooking. This classic dish would certainly have been part of her repertoire, as French cuisine was highly regarded during the Downton era, and Mrs. Patmore, as cook to an earl (a rare position for a woman), would likely have learned her skills working under a French chef before arriving at Downton. Serving a French menu was so fashionable at the time that some British dishes were given French names in cookery books just to appear more posh.

SERVES 6

INGREDIENTS

5 tablespoons (40 g) flour

Salt and black pepper

4 whole chicken legs plus 4 thighs, about 5 lb (2.3 kg) total

2 tablespoons unsalted butter (1 tablespoon at room temperature)

10 small shallots or 20 pearl onions, peeled and left whole

¼ lb (115 g) bacon slices, cut into ½-inch (12-mm) pieces

1 bottle (750 ml) dry red wine

Bouquet garni of 2 fresh flat-leaf parsley sprigs, 2 fresh thyme sprigs, and 1 bay leaf, tied into a bundle with kitchen string

9 oz (250 g) small button mushrooms, brushed clean and sliced

Chopped fresh flat-leaf parsley, for garnish

Preheat the oven to 325°F (165°C). Put 4 tablespoons (30 g) of the flour into a shallow bowl and season with salt and pepper. Dust the chicken pieces with the seasoned flour, coating evenly and tapping off the excess.

In a large, heavy ovenproof pot, melt 1 tablespoon of the butter over medium heat. Add the shallots and cook, stirring, about 3 minutes. Add the bacon and continue to cook, stirring, until the shallots are caramelized and the bacon is crisp, about 5 minutes. Using a slotted spoon, transfer the shallots and bacon to a plate.

Working in batches to avoid crowding, add the chicken pieces to the fat remaining in the pot and cook over medium heat, turning once, until golden brown, 5–8 minutes on each side. As each batch is ready, transfer the pieces to a plate. When all the chicken is browned, return the shallots and bacon to the pot. Pour in the wine, stir with a wooden spoon to loosen any bits on the pot bottom, and carefully add the chicken pieces, bouquet garni, and mushrooms. Bring to a simmer and simmer for 10 minutes, then cover, transfer to the oven, and cook until the chicken is so tender it is nearly falling from the bone, about 1 hour.

Remove the pot from the oven and, using a slotted spoon, transfer the chicken to a plate. Cover with aluminum foil to keep warm. In a small bowl, make a beurre manié by working together the remaining 1 tablespoon each flour and butter with a fork to a smooth paste. Place the pot on the stove top and bring to a boil over medium heat. Gradually whisk in the beurre manié, a nugget at a time. Adjust the heat and simmer until the liquid thickens, about 15 minutes. Rewarm the chicken in the liquid, garnish with parsley, and serve.

MADRAS CHICKEN CURRY

This recipe appears in the 1932 book *Good Things in England*, written by Florence White, a noted collector of English folk cookery. White credits the recipe to Colonel A. R. Kenney-Herbert, who served in the British army in India, where he was stationed in Madras (now Chennai) from the late 1850s to the early 1890s and who penned numerous articles on Indian cookery for both Indian and British newspapers. A true dish of Madras-style chicken would have respected South Asian cooking techniques and called for a more complex combination of seasonings than what the colonel suggested, but he knew he had to simplify both the preparation and the flavors for his audience. In the Downton era, this curry would have likely been served as a side dish, but when accompanied with rice, it makes a good main course.

SERVES 6

INGREDIENTS

⅔ cup (160 ml) whole milk

2 tablespoons ground dessicated coconut or almond meal

¼ cup (30 g) flour

Salt and black pepper

4 whole chicken legs plus 4 thighs, about 5 lb (2.3 kg) total

2 tablespoons unsalted butter

¼ lb (115 g) shallots, chopped

1 tablespoon Madras curry powder

1 tablespoon Indian red curry paste

1 tablespoon unsweetened tamarind concentrate

1 teaspoon sugar

1¼ cups (300 ml) chicken stock

Cooked white rice, for serving

In a small saucepan, combine the milk and ground coconut over medium heat and bring to a simmer, stirring occasionally. Remove from the heat and leave to infuse until needed.

Put the flour into a shallow bowl and season with salt and pepper. Dust the chicken pieces with the seasoned flour, coating evenly and tapping off the excess.

In a large, heavy pot, melt 1 tablespoon of the butter over medium heat. Add the shallots and cook, stirring occasionally, until golden, about 5 minutes. Meanwhile, in a small bowl, mix together the curry powder, curry paste, tamarind, sugar, 1 teaspoon salt, and 1 tablespoon of the stock. When the shallots are golden, add the curry powder mixture and cook, stirring constantly, until the liquid is reduced by two-thirds, about 7 minutes. Be careful the mixture does not burn. (This step is similar to making a roux.) Remove from the heat, scoop the shallot mixture into a small bowl, and reserve.

Return the pot to medium heat and add the remaining 1 tablespoon butter. When the butter melts and begins to bubble, add the chicken pieces, in batches to avoid crowding, and cook, turning as needed, until nicely browned on all sides, 5–8 minutes on each side. As each batch is ready, transfer it to a plate.

When all the pieces are browned, return them to the pot and add the reserved shallot mixture followed by the rest of the stock. Bring to a simmer over medium heat, stirring occasionally to distribute the shallot mixture evenly, then remove from the heat and let stand for 30 minutes.

Return the pot to the stove top over medium heat, bring back to a simmer, and stir in the milk mixture. Simmer until the chicken is cooked through but not falling off the bone, 30–45 minutes.

To serve, transfer the curry to a warmed serving dish and offer the rice on the side.

FOOD FOR THOUGHT

Recipes for curry have been included in English cookery books since the mid-1700s, but they were never meant to represent authentic Indian dishes. During their time on the subcontinent, British colonists grew to appreciate the milder-spiced stews and braises, which they dubbed curry, an anglicized form of *kari*, or "sauce," in Tamil, a language spoken primarily in southern India and northern Sri Lanka. When they returned to Britain, they brought with them a taste for an array of exotic spices—cardamom, cumin, turmeric, ginger, and more—which were soon combined into a prepackaged mix that became known as curry powder. The English quickly embraced the new seasoning, and by 1810, the first Indian restaurant in London, the Hindoostane Coffee House, opened at 34 George Street, in Mayfair. Anglo-Indian fusion cuisine was born and has remained hugely popular to this day.

TAMARIND CURRY OF RABBIT WITH RHUBARB

This recipe comes from *The Cookery Book of Lady Clark of Tillypronie* (née Charlotte Coltman), a large, comprehensive volume of Victorian recipes, all of them tested by the ladyship herself. Many of the recipes note from whom and when she collected them. This dish, which lists the source as Mr. Baker in the year 1891, appears in the chapter dedicated to curries, and although it is made with rabbit, it is equally good prepared with chicken. Lady Clark remarks this curry is at its best after three days. She was right.

SERVES 4

INGREDIENTS

I rabbit or chicken, about 2¾ lb (1.2 kg), cut into serving pieces

3 tablespoons flour

I tablespoon curry powder

I tablespoon unsalted butter

2 yellow onions, chopped

I carrot, peeled and chopped

7 oz (200 g) rhubarb, trimmed and chopped, or 2 cooking apples, halved, cored, and chopped

Juice of I lemon

4½ cups (1.1 l) chicken stock

FOR THE SAUCE

I tablespoon unsalted butter

4 yellow onions, chopped

I tablespoon garam masala

I tablespoon flour

I teaspoon mango chutney

I tablespoon unsweetened tamarind concentrate

Cooked white rice, for serving

If using rabbit, put the pieces into a large bowl of liberally salted water, cover, and refrigerate overnight to rid the rabbit of any residual blood. Drain and dry the pieces before cooking. Skip this step if using chicken.

Preheat the oven to 325°F (165°C).

Mix together the flour and curry powder in a shallow bowl. Dust the rabbit pieces with the seasoned flour, coating evenly and tapping off the excess. In a large, heavy ovenproof pot, melt the butter over medium heat. When the butter melts and begins to bubble, add the rabbit pieces, in batches to avoid crowding, and cook, turning as needed, until nicely browned on all sides, 5–8 minutes on each side. As each batch is ready, transfer it to a plate.

When all the pieces are browned, return them to the pot and toss in the onions, carrot, rhubarb, and lemon juice. Pour in the stock and bring to a simmer over medium heat. Cover the pot, transfer it to the oven, and braise the rabbit for 1½ hours. The rabbit meat should be just falling from the bone.

Remove the pot from the oven and, using a large slotted spoon, transfer the rabbit to a plate. Cover with aluminum foil to keep warm. Pass the contents of the pot through a fine-mesh sieve placed over a bowl and discard the solids. Measure 3½ cups (825 ml) of the liquid and set aside for the sauce.

To make the sauce, in a deep, heavy saucepan, melt the butter over medium heat. Add the onions and cook, stirring occasionally, until golden, about 5 minutes. Add the garam masala, flour, chutney, and tamarind and cook, stirring constantly, until the mixture turns a rich brown, 1–2 minutes. Be careful it does not burn. (This step is similar to making a roux.) Slowly pour in the 3½ cups (825 ml) rabbit cooking liquid while stirring constantly, then bring to a simmer over medium-low heat and simmer until reduced and thickened to a nice sauce consistency, about 20 minutes.

Just before serving, rewarm the rabbit in the sauce, then transfer the curry to a warmed serving dish and offer the rice on the side.

MARY: *In the whole year, we fend for ourselves at Christmas lunch and on New Year's Eve. It doesn't seem much to me.*

CARLISLE: *You haven't had to fight for what you've got.*

MARY: *Oh do try to get past that. It makes you sound so angry all the time.*

~ SEASON 2, EPISODE 9

VIOLET

It seems a pity to miss such a good pudding.

~ SEASON 3, EPISODE 6

MEAT PIES & SAVORY PUDDINGS

GAME BIRD PIE

While the recipe from which this one is adapted calls for grouse, not everyone who hopes to dine as the Crawleys do in *Downton Abbey* is able to acquire these small game birds. In England, grouse live mostly in the north, especially in Yorkshire, where the series is set. They are also common in Scotland, where the author of *The Dudley Book of Cookery and Household Recipes*, the source of the original pie, lived in the late nineteenth and early twentieth century. The pie can be served hot or cold, though Lady Dudley fails to mention that you should add a jelly if serving it cold. She also doesn't include any spices, so a few that would be appropriate for this type of pie have been added here. If you decide to serve the pie cold, a green salad is the best accompaniment, especially when made from watercress, which would have been favored, along with young leaves of plants from the greenhouse, at Downton.

SERVES 4–6

INGREDIENTS

FOR THE FILLING

6 chicken eggs, or 12 quail eggs

9 oz (250 g) brown mushrooms

2 tablespoons unsalted butter

Salt and black pepper

5½ oz (155 g) thin bacon slices

7 oz (200 g) boneless grouse, chicken, or pheasant meat, ground, or chicken livers, chopped

Ground mace, for sprinkling

Ground allspice or cloves, for sprinkling

2 tablespoons chopped fresh flat-leaf parsley

6 boneless grouse breasts, chicken breasts, or pheasant breasts, about 2½ lb (1.1 kg) total

1½ cups (350 ml) tawny port

FOR THE PASTRY

3⅓ cups (415 g) all-purpose flour, plus more for the work surface

3⅓ cups (415 g) bread flour

1 egg, lightly beaten

½ cup (115 g) unsalted butter, at room temperature, cut into several pieces

1¼ cups (300 ml) water

5½ oz (155 g) lard, at room temperature

1½ teaspoons sea salt

1 egg yolk beaten with 1 tablespoon whole milk, for egg wash

IF SERVING COLD

1¾ cups (425 ml) game, veal, or chicken stock

2 teaspoons powdered gelatin, or 4 gelatin sheets

This pie can be made in a 4½-lb (2-kg) game pie mold or a 7¼-inch (18.5-cm) round springform pan with 3¼-inch (8-cm) sides.

Before you begin making the pastry, prepare the eggs and the mushrooms for the filling. Boil the eggs in water to cover until they are not quite hard-boiled but are hard enough to peel easily. Brush the mushrooms clean, then trim the stem ends and slice the mushrooms ¼ inch (6 mm) thick. In a frying pan, melt the butter over medium heat. Add the mushrooms and cook, stirring occasionally, until browned on both sides and just tender, about 5 minutes. Season with salt and pepper. Set the eggs and mushrooms aside until needed. Ready all of the remaining filling ingredients.

To make the pastry, in a large bowl, whisk together the flours. Add the egg and mix just until it is loosely mixed in with the flours, then scatter the butter pieces on top. In a small saucepan, combine the water, lard, and salt and place over high heat. As soon as the mixture begins to bubble, remove the pan from the heat and let stand just until the lard has melted.

The lard mixture should still be very hot. If it isn't, return it to the stove top and bring it to a bare simmer. Pour the hot lard mixture over the butter and flour and, using a wooden spoon or silicone spatula, mix everything together until a shaggy mass forms. Once the mixture is cool enough to touch with your hands, turn it out onto a work surface and knead until a smooth, soft dough forms. This should take no more than 3–5 minutes. The dough must still be warm when you shape it.

Cut off one-third of the dough for the lid, wrap it in plastic wrap, and set it in a warm spot, such as on the stove or a radiator.

If you are using a game pie mold, on a lightly floured work surface, roll out the remaining pastry into an ellipse about ⅓ inch (8 mm) thick and large enough to line the bottom and sides of the mold with at least ¾–1 inch (2–2.5 cm) overhanging the sides. Center the mold on top of the pastry and cut 2 triangles about 4 inches (10 cm) wide on each end. Remove the mold. Fold both ends of the pastry into the middle, then carefully lift the pastry and place it on the bottom of the mold (you don't need to grease the mold because the pastry contains enough fat). Open out the pastry and press it gently onto the bottom and up the sides of the mold, making sure there is overhang for attaching the lid later. Push the edges of the ends together where you cut the triangles to create a neat seam. If there are cracks or holes, you can repair them with any leftover pastry, providing it is still warm enough to adhere. Trim the excess pastry overhanging the rim to ¾ inch (2 cm), then gather up the pastry scraps, press them together, wrap in plastic wrap, and reserve for making decorations.

If you are using a springform pan, shape the warm pastry into a round chunk, set it on a work surface, and then start pushing up on the pastry as if you are making a small bowl. When you have a rough bowl shape, set the pastry in the pan and, using your fingers, press the pastry from the middle of the bottom toward and then up the sides of the pan. The base and sides will become thinner as you continue to push the pastry out and up. Check around the rim of the pan base to make sure the pastry is not too thick in that area and press to thin if needed. The great thing is that you can keep molding the pastry until it covers the base and the sides of the pan evenly. If there are cracks or holes, you can repair them with any leftover pastry, providing it is still warm enough to adhere.

Recipe continues

In season 1, episode 6, the Dowager Countess says, "We'll give her (Lady Mary) till the start of the grouse." The phrase "the start of the grouse" refers to the start of the grouse hunting season on August 12, also known as Glorious Twelfth. As hunting was such a big part of the lives of the upper class, it comes as no surprise that the opening days of various game seasons were signature dates on the annual calendar.

The hunting party could not know if what they were shooting were young grouse or old grouse, so Mrs. Patmore would have had to adapt her menu depending on what was brought to the kitchen. While a young bird needed only a short time on top of the stove or in the oven, older birds called for long, slow cooking in stews or in pies.

Today, grouse are quite expensive because managing their habitat is costly: two birds "need four to five acres of heather to live and brood," according to Richard Townsend of Yorkshire Game, a processor of wild game and venison. That diet of heather is what gives them them their distinctive and highly prized taste.

The base and sides should be about ⅓ inch (8 mm) thick. Trim the excess pastry overhanging the rim to ¾ inch (2 cm) to use for attaching the lid. Gather up the pastry scraps, press them together, wrap in plastic wrap, and reserve for making decorations.

Preheat the oven to 375°F (190°C). Line a sheet pan with parchment paper.

Arrange the bacon slices crosswise along the bottom and up the sides of the pastry-lined mold, allowing the ends of the slices to hang over the sides of the mold so they can be folded over once the mold is filled. Spread half of the ground meat or chopped livers evenly over the bacon-lined base, then sprinkle with a pinch each of pepper, mace, and allspice. Arrange the eggs on top. You can chop them but leaving them whole creates a prettier result. Sprinkle half of the parsley over the eggs, then spread the mushrooms evenly over the top.

Arrange half of the grouse breasts on top and sprinkle with a pinch each of pepper, mace, and allspice. Add the remaining ground meat or chopped livers, followed by the last of the grouse breasts. Pour the port evenly over the breasts, then fold the ends of the bacon slices over the top. Clean the work surface, then roll out the pastry for the lid into an ellipse if using a game pie mold or a round if using a springform pan. It should be ⅓ inch (8 mm) thick and about 1½ inches (4 cm) larger than the top of the mold. Using a small, sharp knife, cut a hole about ¾ inch (2 cm) in diameter in the center. Fold the pastry overhang around the rim inward and brush with the egg wash. Place the lid on top and crimp together the lid and bottom crust all around, sealing the edges well. Using a pastry strip ⅓ inch (8 mm) wide, create a rim around the hole in the lid, attaching it with a bit of egg wash. This will act like a chimney, preventing any liquid from seeping out of the lid and making the jelly easier to add, if using.

To decorate the top of the pie, roll out the leftover pastry about ⅛ inch (3 mm) thick and cut out small shapes. Leaf shapes were popular, and you can cut out simple ellipses or use a special cutter to create ivy or holly. Brush the top of the pie with the egg wash, add the decorations, and then give the decorations a good coating of the egg wash as well. Reserve the remaining egg wash for use later.

FOOD FOR THOUGHT

Game birds have a characteristic flavor that is enhanced by hanging the meat for a period of time. At Downton Abbey, all game meat would be hung in the game larder, a cold room with good air circulation. How long birds are left to hang depends on their species, age, and weather conditions. For example, older birds are left for two to four days in the autumn, while they can be left for fourteen to eighteen days in the freezing temperatures of winter.

Young grouse or snipe, another favorite game bird of the Edwardian era, are usually eaten soon after they are shot, especially at the start of the season in August, which is still full summer. The season for partridge, Scottish woodcock, duck, goose, and moorhen starts in September, with pheasant and English woodcock following from October. By February 1, all the game bird seasons are over.

Luckily for hunters, when the game bird seasons are finished, there are still plenty of deer to shoot, as at least one species is always in season during the year.

Place the pie on the prepared sheet pan and slide the pan into the oven. Bake for 1½–2 hours. It is ready when an instant-read thermometer inserted through the hole in the lid to the center registers 165°F (74°C) or higher.

If you are serving the pie warm, you can give the sides of the pie a coating of egg wash to glaze them. To do so, remove the pie from the oven and let it rest for 15 minutes. While it rests, increase the oven temperature 400°F (200°C). Then, carefully and slowly, unclasp and lift off the sides of the mold. Brush the egg wash on the sides of the pie and return it to the oven for 5 minutes. When the pie is ready, carefully transfer it to a serving plate and, using a sharp knife, cut into wedges or slices.

If serving the pie cold, let cool to room temperature, cover loosely with a kitchen towel, and refrigerate in the mold overnight. To glaze the sides of the pie before serving, preheat the oven to 400°F (200°C). With the chilled mold still on the sheet pan, uncover the pie, carefully and slowly unclasp and lift off the sides of the mold, and brush the sides of the pie with the egg wash. When the oven is ready, place the pie in the oven for 5 minutes, then remove from the oven and set aside.

To make the jelly, set aside ¼ cup (60 ml) of the stock in a small bowl if using powdered gelatin and pour the remaining stock into a saucepan. Sprinkle the gelatin over the stock in the small bowl and let stand until softened, 3–5 minutes. If using gelatin sheets, pour all the stock into a saucepan, then put the sheets into a bowl, add water to cover, and let soak until floppy, 5–10 minutes. Bring the stock in the saucepan to a boil and remove from the heat. If using powdered gelatin, add the softened gelatin and its stock to the hot stock in the saucepan and stir until dissolved. If using gelatin sheets, lift the sheets from the water, wring gently to release excess water, add to the stock, and stir until the gelatin dissolves. Let the stock cool until the jelly is gloopy. Then slowly, bit by bit, pour it into the pie through the steam hole. When all the jelly has been added, re-cover the pie with the towel and refrigerate for at least 2 hours before serving to allow the jelly to set. When the pie is ready, carefully transfer it to a serving plate and, using a sharp knife, cut into wedges or slices.

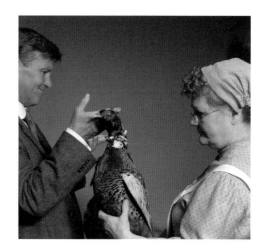

MRS. PATMORE: *I had to get out of that kitchen if I'm not to be found dead under the table.*

~ SEASON 2, EPISODE 4

THE FOX HUNT

There are two scenes in which Lord Grantham is hosting a fox hunt. We see the Earl and others officiating at the hunt clad in red coats, while Mary, as a rider participating in the field, is wearing black.

The origin of the modern fox hunt we see at Downton dates to the eighteenth century, when the aristocrat Hugo Meynell, a country landowner, bred a hound of remarkable speed, stamina, and scenting powers that could successfully pursue the quick and wily fox. He then combined his new hounds with horses and his fellow aristocrats and an upper-class sport was born. The hounds chased the foxes, and the party had to try and keep up with them, facing the many obstacles the British countryside brings: hedges, fences, stone walls, and streams. For example, in season 1, episode 3, we see Lady Mary and Mr. Pamuk going over a fence and through water. The real sport was to know your horse and to master the rough and often dangerous terrain, not the killing of the fox.

Many aristocratic families faced economic difficulties after World War I and could no longer afford to host a proper hunt. We know the Crawleys experienced financial setbacks as well, but the Earl continues to hold hunts as a matter of pride and tradition. Money troubles were not the only thing working against fox hunting, however. Many ethical concerns existed even in the time of Downton, as the fox was taken down by the many dogs or put out of its misery by a gun. Yet it would take until 2005 for the sport to be officially banned in England.

ROBERT: *Do you really like riding like that? When a side-saddle is so much more graceful?*

MARY: *And so much more dangerous.*

~ SEASON 6, EPISODE 1

YORKSHIRE CHRISTMAS PIE

In 1858, a Yorkshire Christmas pie was served to Queen Victoria at Windsor Castle. The pie was beautifully decorated but also of such enormous size that it had to be carried into the room on the shoulders of four footmen. Although not all Yorkshire Christmas pies were so large, they were a status symbol because of the expensive ingredients used. This was also true in the seventeenth century, as illustrated by these few lines from Robert Herrick's poem "Christmas Eve": "Come guard this night the Christmas-Pie, / That the thief, though ne'er so sly, / With his flesh-hooks, don't come nigh, / To catch it." A French visitor of the same period noted that the pie contained beef, fowl, eggs, sugar, currants, citrus, and an array of spices.

While the French traveler mentioned beef in the pie, goose was the more common choice for large Christmas pies. In the eighteenth century, Yorkshire pies were made by stuffing a turkey with smaller birds, one inside another, and then sewing the birds closed, much like the contemporary turducken. Here, filleted meat and poultry have been used for ease.

SERVES 8–10

INGREDIENTS

FOR THE FILLING

1 lb (450 g) boneless, skinless chicken breasts

¾ lb (340 g) boneless, skinless partridge breasts

10½ oz (300 g) boneless, skinless pheasant breasts

3 oz (90 g) boneless, skinless quail breast

2 wild hare saddles, about 9 oz (250 g) total (or additional poultry breasts)

2½ tablespoons ground mace

2 tablespoons ground nutmeg

3½ teaspoons ground cloves or allspice

2 tablespoons plus ¾ teaspoon black pepper

6½ tablespoons (100 ml) Madeira or sherry

1 lb (450 g) ground meat, such as veal, pork, lamb, or poultry

2 tablespoons finely chopped fresh flat-leaf parsley

2 teaspoons finely chopped fresh thyme

Pinch of sea salt

3½ oz (100 g) thin bacon slices

FOR THE PASTRY

3⅓ cups (415 g) all-purpose flour, plus more for the work surface

3⅓ cups (415 g) bread flour

1 egg, lightly beaten

½ cup (115 g) unsalted butter, at room temperature, cut into several pieces

1¼ cups (300 ml) water

5½ oz (155 g) lard, at room temperature

1½ teaspoons sea salt

1 egg yolk beaten with 1 tablespoon whole milk, for egg wash

To begin the filling, in a large, deep bowl, combine the chicken, partridge, pheasant, quail, and hare. Sprinkle with the mace, nutmeg, cloves, and pepper and turn to coat the meats evenly with the spices. Pour the Madeira over the mixture, turn to coat evenly, and then cover and refrigerate for at least a few hours or preferably overnight.

The day of baking, in a bowl, combine the ground meat, parsley, thyme, and salt and mix well. Rinse the marinade off the poultry and hare and pat them dry with paper towels. Have the bacon ready.

Position a rack in the lower third of the oven and preheat to 375°F (190°C). Line a sheet pan with parchment paper. Have ready a 4½-lb (2-kg) game pie mold.

Recipe continues

To make the pastry, in a large bowl, whisk together the flours. Add the egg and mix just until it is loosely mixed in with the flours, then scatter the butter pieces on top. In a small saucepan, combine the water, lard, and salt and place over high heat. As soon as the mixture begins to bubble, remove the pan from the heat and let stand just until the lard has melted.

The lard mixture should still be very hot. If it isn't, return it to the stove top and bring it to a bare simmer. Pour the hot lard mixture over the butter and flour and, using a wooden spoon or silicone spatula, mix everything together until a shaggy mass forms. Once the dough is cool enough to touch with your hands, turn it out onto a work surface and knead until a smooth, soft dough forms. This should take no more than 3–5 minutes. The dough must still be warm when you roll it out.

Cut off one-third of the dough for the lid, wrap it in plastic wrap, and set it in a warm spot, such as on the stove or a radiator. On a lightly floured work surface, roll out the remaining pastry into an ellipse about ⅓ inch (8 mm) thick and large enough to line the bottom and sides of the mold with at least ¾–1 inch (2–2.5 cm) overhanging the sides. Center the mold on top of the pastry and cut 2 triangles about 4 inches (10 cm) wide on each end. Remove the mold. Fold both ends of the pastry into the middle, then carefully lift the pastry and place it on the bottom of the mold (you don't need to grease the mold because the pastry contains enough fat). Open out the pastry and press it gently onto the bottom and up the sides of the mold, making sure there is overhang for attaching the lid later. Push the edges of the ends together where you cut the triangles to create a neat seam. If there are cracks or holes, you can repair them with any leftover pastry, providing it is still warm enough to adhere. Trim the excess pastry overhanging the rim to ¾ inch (2 cm), then gather up the pastry scraps, press them together, wrap in plastic wrap, and reserve for making decorations.

When the pastry is nicely lining the mold, scoop up half of the ground meat mixture and spread it evenly over the bottom of the pastry crust. Top with the breast fillets of the smallest bird, followed by the second smallest, and then cover with a layer of the bacon slices. Layer the remaining poultry fillets on top,

Why and exactly when the Christmas pie became known as the Yorkshire Christmas pie is unclear, but an 1824 issue of *The Gentleman's Magazine* indicates the name change was deserved: "Yorkshire seems to preserve the festivities of Christmas with more splendour and ancient hospitality than any other part of Great Britain." The author goes on to say higher-class visitors to homes were served Yorkshire Christmas pies while "more humble ones are tendered yule-cake, or bread and cheese."

As *Downton Abbey* is set in the beautiful landscape of Yorkshire, this pie would surely not be missing from the dining table. But it would also have been eaten as part of a Christmas shooting lunch.

separating each layer with a layer of bacon slices. Place a hare saddle to either side of the poultry to fill the gap that has formed, then cover everything with the remaining ground meat mixture. The filling should be higher than the edge of the mold so the finished pie will be domed on top.

Clean the work surface, then roll out the pastry for the lid into an ellipse about ⅓ inch (8 mm) thick and about 1½ inches (4 cm) larger than the top of the mold. Using a small, sharp knife, cut a hole about ¾ inch (2 cm) in diameter in the center. Fold the pastry overhang around the rim inward and brush with the egg wash. Place the lid on top and crimp together the lid and bottom crust all around, sealing the edges well. Using a pastry strip ⅓ inch (8 mm) wide, create a rim around the hole in the lid, attaching it with a bit of egg wash. This will act like a chimney, preventing any liquid from seeping out of the lid.

To decorate the top of the pie, roll out the leftover pastry about ⅛ inch (3 mm) thick and cut out small shapes, such as leaves. Use a little of the egg wash to attach each decoration to the lid. Do not brush the lid of the pie yet. Reserve the remaining egg wash for use later.

Place the pie on the prepared sheet pan and slide the pan into the oven. Reduce the oven temperature to 325°F (165°C) and bake the pie for about 4 hours. It is ready when an instant-read thermometer inserted through the hole in the lid to the center registers 165°F (74°C) or higher.

Remove the pie from the oven. Now, be brave: remove the pie from the mold by unclasping and lifting off the sides. Brush the remaining egg wash over the top and sides of the pie. Return the pie to the oven and bake until the pastry is nicely glazed, 15–30 minutes.

The pie was traditionally allowed to cool completely before transferring to a platter, slicing, and serving, but it is also very good eaten warm. Just leave it to rest for about 15 minutes before cutting into it. When eaten cold, add the jelly from the recipe on page 106.

HENRY: *What is your enthusiasm? Horses?*

MARY: *No. I ride. I even hunt. But I don't see horses in my dreams.*

HENRY: *What then?*

MARY: *I like my work.*

~ SEASON 6, EPISODE 4

BOAR'S HEAD PIE

Nineteenth-century author Charles Francatelli, who was a chef to noblemen and to Queen Victoria in the early 1840s, gives a recipe for boar's head in *The Modern Cook,* his popular collection of French-inspired dishes that was published in 1846. The recipe calls for brining and boning a pig's head and then stuffing it with forcemeat, pistachios, tongue, bacon, and truffles. He starts his recipe with "Procure the head of a bacon hog, which must be cut off deep into the shoulders. . . ." Although regarded as a highly festive dish, it likely didn't look very appealing until it was decorated, so much so that Mrs. Beeton decided not to include a recipe for it when she penned her first book fifteen years later.

Because it can be challenging not only to procure a pig's head but also to find the courage to bone it, cook it, and then stuff it, here only the stuffing is made, which is then encased in a hot-water crust. The recipe comes from *The Modern Baker, Confectioner and Caterer,* a multivolume work edited by John Kirkland and first published in the early 1900s.

SERVES 6–8

INGREDIENTS

FOR THE FILLING

I carrot, peeled and roughly chopped

I yellow onion, roughly chopped

3 fresh thyme sprigs

3 fresh rosemary sprigs

2 quarts (2 l) water

I calf's tongue, about 1½ lb (680 g)

6 cups (250 g) fresh bread crumbs

4½ lb (2 kg) ground pork or pork sausage meat

2 eggs, lightly beaten

2 cloves garlic, finely minced

2 tablespoons minced fresh flat-leaf parsley

2 tablespoons ground marjoram

I teaspoon ground mace

Salt and black pepper

½ cup (60 g) pistachios

2 tablespoons unsalted butter

1¼ lb (570 g) brown or white mushrooms, brushed clean and sliced

8–9 bacon slices (9–10 oz/ 250–285 g)

FOR THE PASTRY

3⅓ cups (415 g) all-purpose flour, plus more for the work surface

3⅓ cups (415 g) bread flour

I egg, lightly beaten

½ cup (115 g) unsalted butter, at room temperature, cut into several pieces

1¼ cups (300 ml) water

5½ oz (155 g) lard, at room temperature

1½ teaspoons sea salt

I egg yolk beaten with I tablespoon whole milk, for egg wash

To make the filling, in a saucepan, combine the carrot, onion, thyme, rosemary, and water. Trim the tongue so you are left with just its clean shape, discarding its tough root. Drop the tongue into the pan (add more water if needed to cover completely) and bring to a boil over high heat. Reduce the heat to maintain a gentle boil and cook for 50–60 minutes. The tongue is ready if when you stick it with a fork and lift it out, it drops from the fork immediately. Let cool until it can be handled, then peel off all the skin. A paring knife can be helpful for this task. Trim away any ragged edges. (If you discover that the skin does not come away easily, return the tongue to the pan and cook for a little longer, then try again.)

In a bowl, soak the bread crumbs in water to cover for about 5 minutes, then drain and squeeze out the excess water.

Recipe continues

In a large bowl, combine the pork, soaked crumbs, eggs, garlic, parsley, marjoram, mace, and I teaspoon each salt and pepper. Mix well, then stir in the pistachios. Cook a nugget of the mixture in a frying pan, then taste and adjust the seasoning.

In a frying pan, melt the butter over medium heat. Add the mushrooms and cook, stirring occasionally, until lightly browned, about 8 minutes. Season with salt and pepper.

Preheat the oven to 375°F (190°C). Line a sheet pan with parchment paper. Line the bottom and the two long sides of a 2-lb (1-kg) loaf pan with parchment paper, allowing the paper to overhang the sides. (The overhang will make it easy to remove the pie from the pan after baking.) The dough is rich in fat so there is no need to grease the pan.

To make the pastry, in a large bowl, whisk together the flours. Add the egg and mix just until it is loosely mixed in with the flours, then scatter the butter pieces on top. In a small saucepan, combine the water, lard, and salt and place over high heat. As soon as the mixture begins to bubble, remove the pan from the heat and let stand just until the lard has melted.

The lard mixture should still be very hot. If it isn't, return it to the stove top and bring it to a bare simmer. Pour the hot lard mixture over the butter and flour and, using a wooden spoon or silicone spatula, mix everything together until a shaggy mass forms. Once the dough is cool enough to touch with your hands, turn it out onto a work surface and knead until a smooth, soft dough forms. This should take no more than 3–5 minutes. The dough must still be warm when you roll it out.

Cut off one-third of the dough for the lid, wrap it in plastic wrap, and set it in a warm spot, such as on the stove or a radiator. On a lightly floured work surface, roll out the remaining pastry into a rectangle about ⅓ inch (8 mm) thick and large enough to line the bottom and sides of the mold with at least ¾–1 inch (2–2.5 cm) overhanging the sides.

Fold the sides and then the ends of the pastry rectangle inward, carefully lift the pastry, and set it on the bottom of the prepared pan. Unfold the ends and then the sides and press the pastry gently onto the bottom and up the sides of the pan, smoothing out any creases and letting the excess pastry overhang the sides.

FOOD FOR THOUGHT

In medieval times, the wild boar played a central role in all the most important celebrations, but especially Christmas. The hunt to secure the coveted holiday game for the table was the pastime of nobles, who, glorying in the danger and adventure that the pursuit entailed, traditionally severed the head of the boar to display as a trophy. Accompanied by trumpeters and much drama, the head was then ceremoniously paraded around the dining hall for all the guests to see. Henry II reportedly even carried the boar's head himself on the occasion of the coronation of his son Henry in 1170. The late fourteenth-century chivalric romance *Sir Gawain and the Green Knight* includes a description of a boar hunt, and Chaucer mentions the custom of serving a boar's head in *The Canterbury Tales*. The dish was also featured in Christmas carols dating back to at least the fifteenth century and as recently as the nineteenth century.

Line the pastry crosswise with half of the bacon slices, allowing the ends of the slices to hang over the sides of the pan. Add one-third of the ground meat mixture and gently press it onto the bottom and halfway up the sides of the pan so there are no holes between the ground meat and the bacon. Spoon all the mushrooms in a layer on top of the meat on the bottom. Place the tongue on top of the mushrooms, then arrange the remaining meat mixture around and on top of the tongue. Finish with a layer of bacon, wrapping the overhanging slices over the top.

Clean the work surface, then roll out the pastry for the lid into a rectangle about ⅓ inch (8 mm) thick and about ½ inch (12 mm) larger than the top of the pan. Using a small, sharp knife, cut two steam holes about ¾ inch (2 cm) in diameter in the middle of the lid, leaving equal space between the holes and the left and right sides. Brush the edges of the bottom crust with the egg wash and place the pastry lid on top. Cut away the excess pastry overhang, then turn the edges under and crimp neatly, sealing the edges well.

To decorate the top of the pie, gather up the pastry scraps, press them together, and then roll out about ⅛ inch (3 mm) thick. Cut out small leaves or other shapes. Brush the top of the pie with the egg wash. Arrange the decorations on top, pressing gently to attach, then brush the decorations with the egg wash.

Place the pie on the prepared sheet pan and slide the pan into the oven. Reduce the oven temperature to 350°F (180°C) and bake for 1½ hours. It is ready when an instant-read thermometer inserted through the hole in the lid registers 185°F (85°C). If not done, cover the top with parchment paper to prevent overbrowning, then return the pie to the oven and continue to bake until it tests done.

If you would like the sides of the pie to be golden brown like the top, using the parchment overhang, lift the pie from the pan 15 minutes before it is ready and set it on a parchment-lined sheet pan. Brush the sides with the egg wash, then slide the pan into the oven and continue baking the pie until it tests done.

When the pie is ready, let it cool completely in the loaf pan or on the sheet pan on a wire rack. If it has not already been removed from the pan, carefully lift it out with the parchment overhang. Cut into thick slices to serve. The pie will keep well covered in the refrigerator for up to 3 days.

THOMAS: *I'm just trying to be helpful.*

MRS. PATMORE: *I'm afraid 'being helpful' is not something we associate you with.*

~ SEASON 2, EPISODE 8

HACKIN PUDDING

This savory pudding of beef, oats, and suet was traditionally served early in the morning on Christmas Day in several counties in northern England. It was boiled in a bag-like intestine or a pudding cloth, then sliced, fried in butter, and served to the male workers of the household. No one remembers the custom today, so we must rely on the literature of the time.

This recipe is adapted from one in Richard Bradley's *The Country Housewife and Lady's Director*, first published in London in 1727, which highlights the importance of having it ready at daybreak: "It is a Custom with us every Christmas-Day in the Morning, to have, what we call an Hackin, for the Breakfast of the young Men who work about our House; and if this Dish is not dressed by that time it is Day-light, the Maid is led through the Town, between two Men, as fast as they can run with her, up Hill and down Hill, which she accounts a great shame."

SERVES 4–6

INGREDIENTS

10½ oz (300 g) lean ground beef or veal

2 eggs, lightly beaten

1 cup (100 g) steel-cut oats, soaked in whole milk to cover overnight and drained

3½ oz (100 g) shredded suet (about ¾ cup)

1 apple, cored and grated

⅓ cup (50 g) dried currants

1 teaspoon sugar

2 teaspoons ground mace

1 teaspoon ground allspice

1 teaspoon chopped candied lemon peel

½ teaspoon salt

Flour, for dusting

Lard or unsalted butter, for frying

In a bowl, combine the beef, eggs, oats, suet, apple, currants, sugar, mace, allspice, candied peel, and salt and mix well.

Drape a kitchen towel or other cloth over a bowl and dust with flour. Shape the beef mixture into a ball and place it in the center of the flour-dusted towel. Bring the edges of the towel up around the ball, twist the towel firmly at the top, and secure the towel in place with kitchen string. Leave the string ends long enough so they can be used for tying the pudding to the saucepan handle.

Bring a large, deep saucepan of water to a boil over high heat. Carefully lower the wrapped pudding into the boiling water so it is fully immersed but is not resting on the bottom of the pan, then tie the string to the handle of the pan to keep the pudding surrounded by water. Alternatively, place an overturned heatproof saucer on the bottom of a large saucepan, place a 4-cup (1-l) pudding mold on the saucer, and put the wrapped pudding in the mold. Fill the pan with water and bring to a boil over high heat.

Cover the pan, adjust the heat to maintain a steady boil, and boil the pudding for 2 hours. Check the water level from time to time and add more boiling water as needed to maintain the original level.

When the pudding is ready, turn off the heat and carefully remove the pudding from the pan. The pudding is at its best when eaten as it was centuries ago: cooled to room temperature, unwrapped, and then sliced about ⅔ inch (1.5 cm) thick and fried in lard or in plenty of butter until richly browned on both sides and warmed through.

YORKSHIRE PUDDING

The earliest puddings in England, such as hackin pudding (see opposite), were savory, but they gradually became sweeter and sweeter, eventually leaving any meat content behind completely. Yorkshire pudding, however, has traditionally contained neither meat nor sugar and can be savory or sweet. Before best-selling cookery book author Hannah Glasse gave the dish its name in 1747, it was known as a dripping pudding because it sat beneath meat as it roasted in the radiant heat of a kitchen fireplace. In those days, it was served before the meat to fill up diners a bit so the more costly roast would stretch further. By the 1920s, it was paired with the meat and the leftovers were sometimes offered at the end of the meal with a little sugar or seasonal fruit.

SERVES 4–6

> **RECIPE NOTE**
>
> A Yorkshire, or dripping, pudding was traditionally made in a large pan, but in the last fifty years or so, it has become fashionable to make individual puddings. Although this recipe uses a large pan, you can instead bake the batter in a Yorkshire pudding pan or a muffin pan, filling each cup no more than half to two-thirds full.

INGREDIENTS

I cup plus 3 tablespoons (280 ml) whole milk

3 eggs

¾ cup plus 2 tablespoons (110 g) flour

Pinch of salt

Sunflower oil or melted clarified butter (see Recipe Note, page 86), lard, or tallow, for the pan

Preheat the oven to 500°F (260°C).

In a bowl, whisk together the milk and eggs until blended. Whisk in the flour and salt until the batter is smooth, making sure it is lump-free.

Pour oil to a depth of ⅜ inch (I cm) into an 8–8½-inch (20–22-cm) round, heavy baking pan or cake pan. Place the pan in the hot oven. At the same time, place a large sheet pan directly under the baking pan to catch any oil spatters, preventing a smoky mess.

When the oil is hot (you will see it spitting), carefully but swiftly pour the batter into the hot oil and close the oven door. Bake the pudding, without opening the oven, until puffed and nicely golden, 20–25 minutes.

To serve, remove the pudding from the oven, immediately cut into wedges, and serve hot.

MRS. PATMORE

Oh! You couldn't be harder on those potatoes if
you wanted them to confess to spying.

~ SEASON 6, EPISODE 4

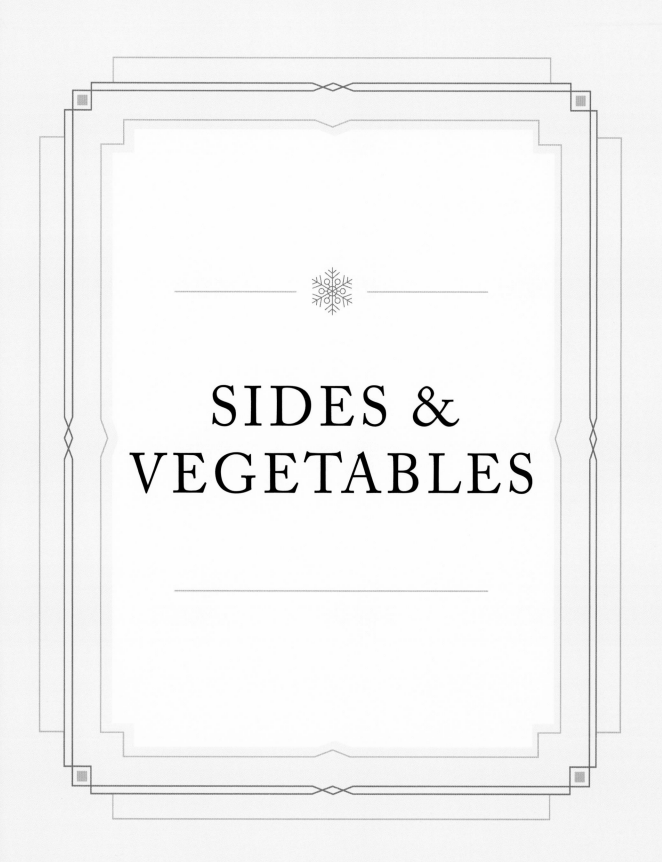

SIDES & VEGETABLES

STEWED FIGS

This easy recipe for citrus-infused stewed figs appears in Eliza Acton's *Modern Cookery*. First published in 1845, the book was wildly popular and a second edition appeared within less than a year. More editions followed, and Acton was on her way to becoming one of the most important food writers of the Victorian era when Isabella Beeton appeared on the scene. Published in 1861, *Mrs Beeton's Book of Household Management* quickly became the textbook of English cookery, pushing *Modern Cookery* into the shadows.

Eliza Acton was actually a poet, not a cook. She started working on *Modern Cookery* at the request of her publisher, who was keen to add a new cookbook to his offerings. The book strongly influenced early food writing, as it was the first to list the ingredients and their amounts separately from the method, something for which Isabella Beeton is usually credited, and to give cooking times. Mrs. Patmore would have had access to these volumes when she was learning to cook. Their likely role in her culinary education also explains why so many of the dishes served at Downton throughout the years come from the Victorian kitchen.

SERVES 6–8

INGREDIENTS

I lemon

I orange

2½ cups (600 ml) water

½ cup (100 g) sugar

I lb (450 g) dried figs, tough stems removed (20–24 figs)

6½ tablespoons (100 ml) port

Using a small, sharp knife, cut a strip of peel from the lemon about ¾ inch (2 cm) wide and 2¾ inches (7 cm) long. Cut a strip of peel the same size from the orange. In a saucepan, combine the water, sugar, and the citrus peels and bring to a simmer over medium heat, stirring to dissolve the sugar. Add the figs and simmer until the figs are plumped and tender, about 20 minutes.

Using a slotted spoon, transfer the figs to a bowl, then continue to simmer the syrup until it is reduced by half, 5–8 minutes. Remove and discard the citrus peels. Halve the lemon and squeeze in the juice, then pour in the port and heat until hot. Do not allow to boil.

If the figs have cooled, pop them back into the syrup and heat just until warm. Arrange the figs in a deep plate or glass dish, as Acton suggests, and pour the syrup over the top. Serve warm.

RECIPE NOTE

Acton suggests placing this dish of figs on the table in the "rice border," indicating exactly where the dish should be set. This Victorian style of serving a meal buffet-style, known as *service à la française*, was obsolete by the Downton years, replaced by courses served in a set order. The figs are a particularly good accompaniment to game, but they can also be served cold for dessert.

PAN POTATOES

Potatoes were ubiquitous on tables throughout Britain in the Downton era, and recipes for them were plentiful. Boiled and roasted were the most popular ways to prepare them, but potato straws, potato waffles, and crisp fried paper-thin slices were also common. During the war years, eating potatoes was encouraged because the British crop was abudant.

Wartime cookery books and Ministry of Food leaflets provided ideas on how to to use potatoes in nearly every way you can imagine. In May Byron's *The Great War Cook Book*, published in 1915, potatoes are featured in nineteen recipes, not including the vegetable and potato chapters. There were even demonstrations on how to use potato flour in place of wheat flour in an attempt to get home cooks to reduce their use of the harder-to-grow grain.

This simple yet beautiful dish comes from Dorothy Allhusen's *A Book of Scents and Dishes*, a striking collection of recipes from upper-class families published in the mid-1920s and sold to raise money for charity. The recipe creates a wonderfully modern potato dish that is a perfect accompaniment to roast meats and fish dishes.

SERVES 4

INGREDIENTS

I lb (450 g) medium-starch potatoes, such as Yukon Gold or Maris Piper (about 2 potatoes)

I clove garlic, halved lengthwise

2 tablespoons olive oil or melted unsalted butter

Salt and black pepper

Preheat the oven to 400°F (200°C).

Using a mandoline or a sharp knife, slice the potatoes crosswise as thinly as possible. Pat the slices dry between sheets of paper towels.

Rub the bottom and sides of a heavy pan 8–8½ inches (20–22 cm) in diameter with the cut sides of the garlic, then discard the garlic. Pour the oil into the pan, add the potato slices, and season with salt and pepper. Using your hands or 2 wooden spoons, turn and mix the slices to coat them on both sides with the oil. Neatly arrange the slices, overlapping them slightly, in layers in the pan, creating a nice-looking pattern.

Bake the potatoes until they are tender and richly browned, 40–45 minutes. The top layer will be crisp and the bottom layer will be soft. Serve warm directly from the pan or turned out onto a serving plate or board.

RECIPE NOTE

At Downton, the potatoes would have been peeled before slicing. It is not necessary, however, and because they are cut very thinly, it is easier to slice them with the skin on. Also, the final presentation is prettier.

TOMATOES À LA BRUXELLES

Stuffed tomatoes were frequently served alongside meat in the Downton era, and Victorian and Edwardian cookery books provided an abundance of recipes for them. They were especially well suited to the *à la russe* style of service common in upper-class homes, in which courses were brought to the table in a prescribed order and portioned by a servant.

For this simple preparation, it is best to use homemade bread crumbs, as store-bought crumbs will typically be too dry, with the exception of *panko* (Japanese bread crumbs), which are stocked in many shops nowadays.

SERVES 6

INGREDIENTS

6 large, firm tomatoes, each about 7 oz (200 g)

1 cup plus 2 tablespoons (120 g) grated Gruyère cheese

¼ cup (30 g) dried bread crumbs

Salt and black pepper

6 eggs

Preheat the oven to 350°F (180°C).

Have ready a large bowl of ice-cold water. Fill a saucepan with water and bring to a boil over high heat. Lightly score an X on the blossom end of each tomato; this will help speed the peeling. Carefully lower 1 or 2 tomatoes into the boiling water and boil for about 15 seconds (start counting when the water begins to bubble again). You should see the skin begin to wrinkle slightly. Using a slotted spoon, transfer the tomatoes to the ice-cold water. As soon as the tomatoes are cool, peel them and then dry them.

Set a fine-mesh sieve over a bowl. Cut a thin slice off the stem end of each tomato, then scoop out the flesh into the sieve, leaving a shell about ⅜ inch (1 cm) thick. Invert the tomatoes onto a paper towel–lined platter or sheet pan to drain while you make the filling.

Allow the tomato flesh to drain briefly, then discard the juice (or reserve for another use). Transfer the flesh to a blender and blend to a purée. Transfer the purée to a bowl, add the cheese and bread crumbs, season with salt and pepper, and mix well to form a thick paste.

Arrange the tomatoes, hollow side up, in a baking dish just large enough to hold them. Crack an egg into each tomato and season with salt and pepper. Carefully spoon the tomato paste on top of the eggs, dividing it evenly.

Bake the tomatoes until the eggs are set, about 30 minutes. Serve warm.

STEWED PRUNES AND CHESTNUTS WITH SHERRY

In *A Century of British Cooking*, the estimable and prolific Marguerite Patten writes that stewed prunes "were regarded as food for the nursery" in the first decade of the twentieth century, though this sherry-infused mix of prunes and chestnuts suggests otherwise. The dish is a perfect partner to game meat or to a bread-and-butter pudding or ice cream.

SERVES 6–8

INGREDIENTS

1 lb (450 g) prunes, pitted

14 oz (400 g) jarred or vacuum-packed roasted and peeled whole chestnuts (about 2½ cups)

¼ teaspoon ground cinnamon

1½ cups (350 ml) sherry

In a saucepan, combine the prunes with water to cover and bring to a boil over medium-high heat. Adjust the heat to maintain a simmer and cook until tender but not falling apart, adding more water if needed to keep them covered. The timing will depend on how old your prunes are: the older and drier the prunes, the longer they will take to soften. The prunes are ready when they are soft and plump but still hold their shape.

Drain the prunes and return them to the pan. Add the chestnuts, sprinkle in the cinnamon, and pour in the sherry. Bring to a simmer over medium heat and simmer for 5 minutes. Transfer to a serving bowl and serve hot.

STUFFED MUSHROOMS

These meat-stuffed mushrooms make a great side dish, but they can also be offered as an hors d'oeuvre or as a savory course. Take the time to source perfectly fresh, uniform-size mushrooms for the most attractive presentation. Brown mushrooms will deliver a deeper flavor, but if you can only find white mushrooms, they will still yield a delicious result.

SERVES 4

INGREDIENTS

Unsalted butter, for the parchment

8 uniform-size brown or white mushrooms, about 9 oz (250 g) total

¼ lb (115 g) ground pork or veal

3 tablespoons dried bread crumbs, plus more for topping

1 egg yolk

2 tablespoons chopped fresh flat-leaf parsley, plus whole leaves for garnish

Salt and black pepper

Olive oil, for drizzling

Preheat the oven to 400°F (200°C). Line a sheet pan with parchment paper and butter the paper.

Remove the stem from each mushroom to create space for the stuffing, then brush the mushrooms clean. Place the mushrooms, hollow side up, on the prepared pan.

To make the stuffing, in a bowl, mix together the pork, bread crumbs, egg yolk, and parsley and season with salt and pepper. Divide the stuffing into 8 equal portions, shape each portion into a ball, and then place a ball in the hollow of each mushroom. Drizzle a little oil over each mushroom and sprinkle lightly with bread crumbs.

Bake the mushrooms until the stuffing is cooked through and the mushrooms are tender when pierced with a knife tip, about 20 minutes. Garnish each mushroom with a parsley leaf and serve warm.

ORANGE SALAD WITH KIRSCH AND CURAÇAO

Although bitter oranges—the kind used for making marmalade—were available in Britain in medieval times, sweet oranges were not imported until the late sixteenth century. Their appearance was thanks to the Portuguese, who, upon encountering the fragrant citrus fruits in China, began cultivating them back home in Europe. These exotic imports were costly, of course, which made them beyond the reach of all but the rich. Their rarity also meant they quickly became associated with Christmas.

Long before the Edwardian period, oranges were studded with cloves as both decoration and to give off a festive scent. In *A Book of Scents and Dishes*, author Dorothy Allhusen provides this striking recipe that echoes the exotic past of the orange. It offers a welcome refreshing contrast to all the rich foods on the Christmas table.

SERVES 4–6

INGREDIENTS

6 oranges

1 tablespoon kirsch

1 tablespoon curaçao

2 tablespoons pistachios, chopped

Using a small, sharp knife, cut a thin slice off the top and bottom of an orange. Stand the orange upright and, following the contour of the fruit, slice downward to remove the peel and pith, rotating the orange after each slice. Repeat with the remaining oranges.

Thinly slice the oranges crosswise and arrange the slices on a platter, overlappng them slightly. In a small bowl, stir together the kirsch and curaçao, then sprinkle the mixture evenly over the fruit. Scatter the pistachios on top and serve.

ENDIVES À LA CRÈME

Although the recipe from which this one is adapted does not mention cheese, adding some and placing the endives in the oven to color the top creates a superior dish. This step also allows you to prepare the endives in advance and then add the white sauce and slip the pan into the oven just before you are about to serve the dish. Endives are often called Belgian or Brussels endives (and also witloof) because the area around Brussels traditionally cultivates a lot of the small, pale, bullet-shaped heads of tighty furled, spear-shaped leaves. A Belgian cook would add ham as well as the cheese to the dish, wrapping a slice around each endive before spooning on the sauce.

SERVES 4–8

INGREDIENTS

4 Belgian endives, about 1¼ lb (570 g) total

1 tablespoon unsalted butter, plus more for the pot

1 cup (240 ml) water

FOR THE SAUCE

4 teaspoons unsalted butter

2 tablespoons flour

1½ cups (350 ml) whole milk

½ cup (60 g) grated Gruyère cheese, plus more for finishing (optional)

Pinch of salt

Pinch of white pepper

Pinch of ground nutmeg

1 egg yolk, beaten

Quarter the endives lengthwise, or halve them if you have found only small ones. Butter the bottom and about 4 inches (10 cm) of the sides of a large, heavy pot. Place the pot on the stove top over medium heat and add the butter. When the butter melts, arrange as many endive quarters or halves, cut side down, as will fit in a single layer on the bottom of the pot and and cook, turning once, until they take on some color, about 5 minutes on each side. Transfer the endive pieces to a plate and repeat with the remaining endives. Remove the pot from the heat.

Return all of the endives to the pot and pour in the water. Cut a piece of parchment paper in the shape and slightly larger than the top of the pot and press it into the pot until it nearly touches the endives. Return the pot to the stove top over low heat, cover, and braise the endives until the thickest parts are tender when pierced with a fork, 10–15 minutes. The timing will depend on the size of the endives.

Remove the endives from the pot, pressing out as much of the cooking liquid as they will release without damaging the vegetable, and set aside on a plate. Cover to keep warm. Reserve the cooking liquid, which is full of flavor, for the sauce.

To make the sauce, melt the butter in a saucepan over medium heat. Add the flour and immediately stir with a wooden spoon until well mixed. Reduce the heat to low and continue to stir until the mixture is dry and comes together in a roux. It is ready when the aroma changes from butter and raw flour to the scent of baked biscuits and smells slighty nutty. Do not allow the mixture to color. Remove the pan from the heat and slowly pour in the reserved cooking liquid and then the milk while stirring constantly to prevent lumps from forming. (Removing the pan from the heat for this step ensures better control. If some lumps form, use a handheld mixer to beat the mixture until it is smooth.) Return the pan to medium-low heat and continue to stir until the sauce thickens, about 2 minutes. Add the cheese, if using, and stir until it melts. Season with the salt, pepper, and nutmeg, then taste and adjust the seasoning if needed. Finally, whisk about ¼ cup (60 ml) of the hot sauce into the egg yolk, then whisk the yolk mixture into the sauce until blended.

Transfer the endives to a warmed serving plate, pour the sauce evenly over the top, and serve. Alternatively, preheat the oven to 400°F (200°C). Arrange the braised endives in a single layer in a baking dish, spoon the cheese-enriched sauce over the top, sprinkle with a dusting of cheese, and place in the oven until the top is golden, about 10 minutes. Serve directly from the dish.

CARLISLE: *Why do we have to help ourselves at luncheon?*

ROBERT: *It's a Downton tradition. They have their feast at lunchtime, and we have ours in the evening.*

CARLISLE: *But why can't they have their lunch early and then serve us, like they normally do?*

MARY: *Because it's Christmas Day.*

~ SEASON 2, EPISODE 9

APPLE AND CELERY SALAD

Celery was often used as a salad vegetable in the past. In this no-fuss combination, it is paired with apple and then dressed with mayonnaise. Using a simple mayonnaise dressing for finishing everything from salads to cold cooked meats and vegetables was popular in the Edwardian kitchen. This salad is also good with grated raw celery root or with radishes thinly sliced in half-moons in place of the celery.

SERVES 4

INGREDIENTS

4 ribs celery, including tender, young leaves

1 good eating apple, such as Granny Smith, Cox's Orange Pippin, or Braeburn

1 tablespoon fresh lemon juice

2 tablespoons mayonnaise

1 tablespoon heavy cream

Black pepper

Fresh mint leaves, for garnish (optional)

Using a small, sharp knife, peel away the tough outer strings from each celery rib. Thinly slice the ribs crosswise on the diagonal, then coarsely chop the leaves.

Peel the apple, quarter lengthwise, and cut away the core. Starting from the short side, slice each quarter as thinly as possible. Working quickly, transfer the slices to a bowl and toss them with the lemon juice, coating evenly to prevent browning.

Add the celery slices to the apple slices, then spoon in the mayonnaise and cream. Stir gently to coat the apple and celery. Transfer to a serving bowl, add a few grinds of pepper from a pepper mill, garnish with mint (if using), and serve.

ARTICHOKES GRATIN

Victorians and Edwardians favored nearly any dishes labeled *au gratin*, and cookery books of both eras included instructions for preparing most vegetables in this manner. Look for young artichokes, as older ones do not have enough flesh. Elongated artichokes, which are longer and more tapered than globe artichokes, are the best choice here—Violetta and Siena are two good varieties—but globe artichokes, which are more readily available, can also be used. When done well and with good produce, these artichokes are quite pretty on a serving plate. This preparation is also known as artichokes Mornay or *fonds d'artichauts à la Mornay*.

SERVES 6–8

INGREDIENTS

2 lemons, halved

8 medium-size artichokes, preferably elongated variety

FOR THE SAUCE

1 tablespoon unsalted butter

1 tablespoon flour

6½ tablespoons (100 ml) whole milk

Pinch of salt

Pinch of white pepper

Pinch of ground nutmeg

FOR THE TOPPING

2 tablespoons grated Parmesan cheese

2 tablespoons dried bread crumbs

2 tablespoons finely chopped fresh flat-leaf parsley

About 4 tablespoons (60 g) unsalted butter, cut into 16 small cubes

Fill a large bowl with water, squeeze the juice from 2 lemon halves into the water, and then pop the spent halves into the water.

Pull off all the tough outer leaves from an artichoke. Using a sharp knife, cut off about 1¼ inches (3 cm) from the top (about one-third of the head) to remove the prickly tips. Cut off the base of the stem, leaving about 1¼ inches (3 cm) attached, then cut away the dark green, fibrous outer layer to reveal the vibrant green interior.

Cut the artichoke in half lengthwise and scrape out any hairy parts from both halves. If the purple part is spiky, trim it out as well. Rub all the cut surfaces of the artichoke halves with a lemon half, then slip the artichoke halves into the lemon water to prevent discoloration. Repeat with the remaining artichokes.

Drain the artichokes, transfer them to a large saucepan, add water to cover, and bring to a boil over high heat. Reduce the heat to medium, cover, and cook until tender when pierced with a knife, 10–15 minutes. The timing will depend on the size of the artichokes.

While the artichokes are cooking, position an oven rack in the upper third of the oven and preheat to 400°F (200°C), then prepare the sauce.

Recipe continues

To make the sauce, melt the butter in a small saucepan over medium-low heat. Add the flour and immediately stir with a wooden spoon until well mixed. Reduce the heat to low and continue to stir until the mixture is dry and comes together in a roux. It is ready when the aroma changes from butter and raw flour to the scent of baked biscuits and smells slightly nutty. Do not allow the mixture to color. Remove the pan from the heat and slowly add the milk while stirring constantly to prevent lumps from forming. (Removing the pan from the heat for this step ensures better control. If some lumps form, use a handheld mixer to beat the mixture until it is smooth.) Return the pan to low heat and continue to stir until the sauce thickens to the consistency of canned cold condensed soup, about 2 minutes. It needs to be thicker than the usual white sauce, as you do not want it to drip off the artichokes. Remove from the heat. Season with the salt, pepper, and nutmeg, then taste and adjust the seasoning if needed.

To make the topping, in a small bowl, stir together the Parmesan, bread crumbs, and parsley.

Place the artichokes, cut side up, on a sheet pan. Top each half with a dollop of the sauce, dividing it evenly. Then sprinkle the halves with the topping, dividing it evenly. Finally, place 2 small butter cubes on the topping on each half.

Bake the artichokes until the topping is golden, 15–20 minutes. Transfer to a serving plate and serve warm.

ROSAMUND: *I'm sorry, Mama, but you know me. I have to say what I think.*

~ SEASON 1, EPISODE 7

ON VEGETABLES

When Edward VII assumed the throne in 1901, he brought with him a penchant for everything French, including the cuisine, which set the national tone among the moneyed classes for lighter meals with more vegetables. In *The Book of Vegetable Cookery: Usual and Unusual,* published in 1931, author Erroll Sherson describes how cooks in a variety of European countries traditionally prepared vegetables in the first decades of the twentieth century: the French use butter or olive oil, the Italians prefer olive oil, and the Germans favor lard. Sherson's pronouncements are much too broad, of course, especially as he goes on to write that the British cook just keeps the water tap close. The French culinary term *à l'anglaise* refers to vegetables cooked or served "in the English manner," which means boiled in a lot of water and served without any embellishment—a condescending French assessment based on Victorian cookery done badly.

Sherson also notes that city dwellers weren't always able to find freshly harvested vegetables. Farm produce would frequently arrive in London in poor condition, with carrots already soft, cauliflower spongy, and cabbage wilted. But this wasn't a problem if you lived and worked on an estate like Downton, where fresh vegetables were gathered from the kitchen garden or procured from tenant farmers and local grocers.

In Victorian times, noble houses also often relied on large, boiler-heated greenhouses to provide out-of-season vegetables for the table—a popular way to show off one's wealth at dinner parties. Such extravagance was disappearing by the beginning of the Edwardian era, however, with many aristocrats finding it too costly to maintain such large estates. Even Lord Grantham, who in spring 1920 learns that his massive investment in a North American railroad company is worthless, would find it necessary to rein in the costs at Downton.

Despite increasing financial worries, the Downton table still held many vegetables dishes. The varied and colorful vegetables of the Mediterranean were not yet widely available in England, however, so Mrs. Patmore and her staff had to come up with new ways to serve long-familiar vegetables. Traditionally, their efforts appeared after the showstopper roast meat, though some were served with previous courses as well, such the fish or entrée, the latter usually a wild game or poultry dish.

SPINACH BALLS À L'ITALIENNE

This dish is from Erroll Sherson's well-regarded *The Book of Vegetable Cookery: Usual and Unusual.* In the book, the recipe is titled Spinach Balls à l'Italienne, but in Italy, it goes by two names: in Siena, the balls are called *malfatti*, or "badly made," and in Florence, *gnudi*, or "naked." They were traditionally made with ricotta, but as the cheese was hard to come by in England in Sherson's day, the recipe suggests using a can of Ideal condensed milk. Curd cheese (similar to a low-fat cream cheese) would have been a better substitute, but because the cook would have had to have access to it fresh, the author instead opted for a pantry staple.

The recipe omits flour, which is integral to binding the mixture. Its absence is not uncommon, however, as ingredients were often left out of recipes, assuming the cook would know what to do. Adding flour to bind a mixture or make it drier was a standard technique in kitchens of the era.

MAKES 16 BALLS; SERVES 4

INGREDIENTS

1 tablespoon unsalted butter

18 oz (500 g) spinach, preferably baby spinach, any tough stems removed

4 egg yolks

3 tablespoons condensed milk

¼ cup (30 g) grated Parmesan cheese

½ cup (85 g) semolina flour

¼ teaspoon salt

¼ teaspoon black pepper

FOR SERVING (SEE RECIPE NOTE)

2 tablespoons unsalted butter

Small handful fresh sage leaves

Shaved Parmesan cheese

Melt the butter in a large saucepan over medium heat. Toss the spinach into the pan and turn and fold the leaves until they are soft and shiny, just 2–3 minutes if using baby spinach and a few minutes longer if using older spinach. Transfer the spinach to a sieve held over the sink or a bowl and, using the back of a spoon, press out as much liquid as possible. Dump the spinach onto a cutting board, chop it finely, return it to the sieve, and again press out as much liquid as possible.

In the same saucepan, combine the spinach, egg yolks, condensed milk, cheese, and 2 tablespoons of the semolina and mix well. Season with the salt and pepper. Place over medium heat and cook, stirring continuously, until the moisture has evaporated and the mixture resembles a lumpy purée, about 5 minutes. Spread the spinach mixture out on a plate or sheet pan and let cool.

Once the spinach mixture has cooled, it should be thick enough to shape into balls. Spread the remaining semolina on a large plate or sheet pan. Dust your hands and a spoon with some of the semolina. Divide the spinach mixture into 16 equal portions, then scoop up a portion with the spoon, roll it between your semolina-dusted hands into a ball about 1¼ inches (3 cm) in diameter, toss it with the semolina, coating on all sides, and set aside on a large, flat plate. When all the balls are shaped and coated, cover the plate and refrigerate the balls for at least 1 hour or preferably overnight.

Bring a large saucepan of salted water to a gentle bubble over high heat. Add the balls and cook until they firm up and begin to float on top, about 3 minutes. Using a slotted spoon, scoop them out, drop them into a warmed serving dish, top as directed in the Recipe Note, and serve.

RECIPE NOTE

The original recipe notes to serve the
spinach balls with melted butter and
grated Gruyère cheese; in Italy it is
traditional to top them with sage butter
and shavings of Parmesan cheese, which
is a superior combination. Melt the
butter in a small frying pan over medium
heat, add the sage, and cook until the
butter begins to brown slightly and the
leaves begin to crisp, about 30 seconds.
Pour the butter and sage over the balls,
add a dusting of cheese, and serve.

TURNIP TOPS WITH CROUTONS

Turnip tops, or turnip greens, have a pleasant peppery, mildly bitter flavor. The best leaves are the youngest ones. Older ones are typically quite bitter, which is probably why these greens are often snubbed by diners. Nowadays, it can be difficult to find turnips with their tops still attached, but they're worth the hunt.

At Downton, these greens would have been regularly served because the leaves could be harvested straight from the vegetable beds without removing the turnips from their dark resting place. In southern Italy, cooks prepare *cime di rapa*, or "turnip tops," with olive oil, garlic, and chile. These greens, known as broccoli rabe or rapini in English-speaking countries, are in the same botanical subspecies as turnips; either works here.

The recipe from which this one is adapted suggests serving the greens with croutons, which are a great partner and are included here. It also mentions that the greens can be topped with poached eggs, which would make a wonderful lunch dish but would be out of place for Christmas, where there would be no shortage of protein on the table.

SERVES 6

INGREDIENTS

4½ lb (2 kg) turnip tops, any tough stems removed

2 tablespoons unsalted butter

Salt and black pepper

I cup (240 ml) whole milk or vegetable stock

FOR THE CROUTONS

6 thin slices white bread

2–3 tablespoons unsalted butter

Turnip tops can conceal dirt and grit, so rinse them in plenty of fresh water. Bring a large pot of water to a boil over high heat. Add the turnip tops and boil for 5 minutes, then drain them into a colander but do not dry them. Transfer the greens to a cutting board and chop into ¾-inch (2-cm) pieces.

Before you begin cooking the turnip tops, make the croutons. Cut out a small, neat triangle (about 4 inches/10 cm on each side) from each slice of bread. Melt the butter in a large frying pan over medium heat. Add the triangles and fry, turning as needed, until golden brown on both sides. Set the croutons aside off the heat and keep warm.

In a large, deep saucepan, melt the butter over medium heat. Add the chopped turnip tops, stir to coat with the butter, and season with salt and pepper. When the vegetables start to stick to the pan, add the milk, stir well, and simmer until the liquid has evaporated, 2–5 minutes.

Transfer the greens to a warmed serving plate and arrange the croutons around the rim of the plate, being careful to keep them off the greens or they will turn soggy. Serve warm.

ROASTED PARSNIPS

While parsnips have become a traditional vegetable accompaniment to Sunday roasts and Christmas dinners, they were once traditionally eaten with salt fish on Ash Wednesday and other fast days when consumption of meat was forbidden. In most recipes of the Victorian and Edwardian periods, popular root vegetables are boiled to death and buried in white sauce or simply puréed. On rarer occasions, they are made into fritters, which prove rather tasteless in the case of parsnips, as they have such a delicate flavor. One recipe instructs to cut parsnips into fingers, dip the pieces in melted butter, flour, and superfine sugar, and then fry them in clarified butter. But despite such elaborate fiddling, the parsnips are still missing their potential glory: caramelized and shiny on the outside, warm and tender on the inside, and bursting with flavor in a muted way.

The best parsnips must be near-candied yet still savory. Here is a recipe that would likely be too fancy for Mrs. Patmore but would certainly have crossed Alfred's mind. Although a footman, he dreamed of becoming a chef and leaves Downton in season 4 to attend chef training at London's Ritz hotel.

SERVES 6

INGREDIENTS

---

18 oz (500 g) parsnips	10 fresh thyme sprigs
1 orange	1 fresh rosemary sprig
3 whole cloves	Pinch of salt
1 tablespoon honey	Black pepper
2 tablespoons unsalted butter, melted	

Preheat the oven to 375°F (190°C).

Trim and peel the parsnips, then cut them in half lengthwise. If the parsnips are quite small, you can skip the peeling and leave them whole. Bring a large saucepan of salted water to a boil over high heat. Add the parsnips and boil for 5 minutes if they are small and 10 minutes if they are large. Drain well and pat dry with paper towels.

Using a small, sharp knife, remove the peel from the orange in strips of any size and add the strips to a small saucepan. Halve and squeeze the orange to yield 2 tablespoons juice and add the juice to the pan along with the cloves. Place the pan over medium heat, bring to a simmer, and simmer until the juice is reduced by half. Remove from the heat, remove and discard the cloves and orange peel, and stir in the honey.

In a roasting pan just large enough to hold the parsnips in a single layer, mix together the orange-honey mixture, butter, thyme, rosemary, salt, and two turns of the pepper mill. Toss in the parsnips and use your hands to coat them evenly with the seasoning mixture.

Roast the parsnips until tender when pierced with a knife tip, 30–40 minutes. The timing will depend on their size. Discard the herb sprigs, then transfer the parsnips to a warmed oval serving plate and serve warm.

BRANSON

When is the wedding?

EDITH

*We are thinking Christmas would be fun. Maybe
New Year's Eve, when the decorations are still up.*

~ SEASON 6, EPISODE 9

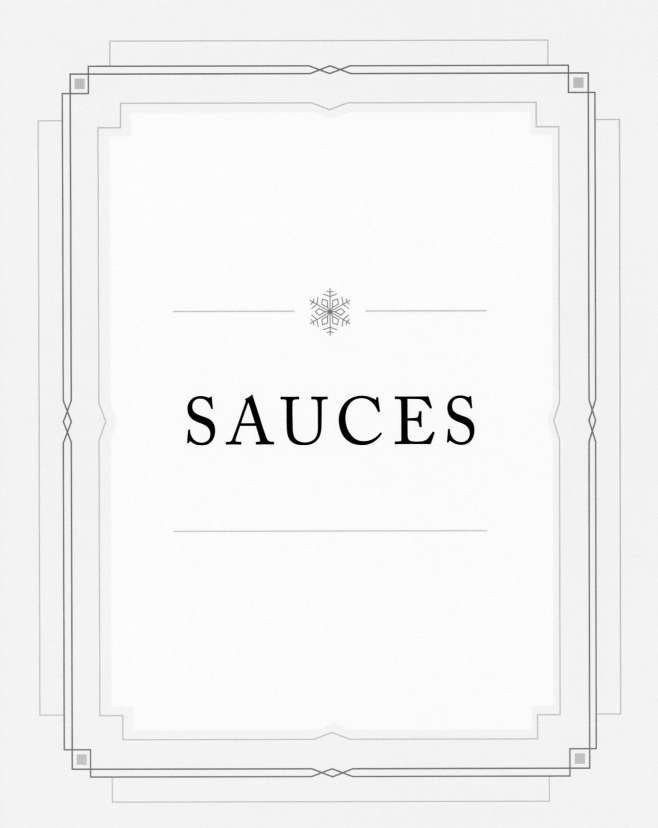

SAUCES

BREAD SAUCE

Thickening sauces with bread dates back to at least the Middle Ages and was common in many places in Europe. But bread sauce itself, which also dates to the medieval period, is nearly unknown outside of Britain, where it has remained a favorite throughout the centuries. Today, people may think of this simple sauce as a humble dish—a way to use up stale bread. But in the past, leftover bread was a luxury in many households, and bread sauce was a dish for people of privilege until into the twentieth century.

This recipe is from *Mrs Beeton's Book of Household Management*, which was first published in 1861 and immediately became a best-seller. Although its author, Isabella Beeton, died in 1865, the book was reprinted and expanded many times, stretching well into the next century and beyond. Mrs. Patmore would have known many of the recipes from this book by heart.

This thick, white sauce is the traditional accompaniment to roast fowl and feathered game, and in the Downton era and modern-day England, it is served with the turkey at Christmas dinner.

MAKES 3 CUPS (ABOUT 700 ML)

INGREDIENTS

2½ cups (600 ml) whole milk

1 large yellow onion, quartered

2 whole cloves

1 blade mace

1 bay leaf

4 black peppercorns

1 allspice berry

¼ lb (115 g) good-quality dense white bread, crusts removed

2 tablespoons unsalted butter

2 tablespoons heavy cream

Salt and black pepper

In a saucepan, combine the milk, onion, cloves, mace, bay leaf, peppercorns, and allspice and bring to a simmer over medium-low heat. Simmer until the onion is tender, about 10 minutes. Remove from the heat and strain the milk through a fine-mesh sieve into a heatproof bowl, discarding the onion and spices. Rinse the pan and reserve.

Break the bread into small pieces, drop them into the hot milk, and let soak for 1 hour.

Pour the bread and milk into the reserved pan and whisk vigorously until creamy and free of lumps. Add the butter and cream and bring to a simmer over low heat, whisking occasionally. Season to taste with salt and pepper.

Serve warm. Or you can make the sauce ahead, let it cool, cover, and refrigerate for up to 2 days. Reheat gently over low heat just until hot.

RECIPE NOTE

Bread sauce should be very thick and pudding-like; however, some people prefer a smoother and more sauce-like bread sauce. If you find the sauce is too thick for your liking, whisk in a tablespoon or two of water to thin it.

BRANDY BUTTER

A quite recent addition to the Christmas food repertoire, brandy butter was served to Queen Alexandra before World War I at the Christmas luncheon at Sandringham, the royal estate in Norfolk. Recipes for brandy butter—also known as hard sauce—appeared in American cookery books in the nineteenth century, but they didn't feature in English recipe books until the twentieth century. A similar mixture of butter enriched with sherry, Madeira, or brandy and flavored with sugar and spices did appear, but the flavorings were simmered in melted butter and the sauce was served with sweet puddings. The rum butter of Cumbria, in north west England, is similar to brandy butter, though it is unclear when it was first made. In recent decades, a couple of unverifiable legends have suggested it dates back to the eighteenth century.

Americans introduced the custom of serving Christmas or plum pudding with brandy butter, and although Cora is of American descent, at Downton the pudding would have been served the traditional way, either plain or with custard sauce.

MAKES ABOUT 1 CUP (250 G)

INGREDIENTS

½ cup plus 1 tablespoon (125 g) unsalted butter, at room temperature

1 cup plus 1 ½ tablespoons (125 g) confectioners' sugar

2 tablespoons boiling water

3 tablespoons brandy

In a bowl, using a wooden spoon (or a handheld mixer), cream together the butter and sugar until smooth and creamy. Add the boiling water and brandy and whisk until smooth. Serve immediately, or cover and refrigerate until serving.

RECIPE NOTE

This sauce typically elicits strong opinions: people either love it or hate it. Should you favor it, the sauce is also good with mince pies.

WINE SAUCE

Recipes for wine sauces are numerous from the fourteenth century onward, all of them quite similar. The differences are primarily the choice of spices and whether or not lemon or orange peel is added to the mix. Although these sauces traditionally accompany sweet dishes, such as plum pudding and figgy pudding, they are equally good with game, where sweetness is often a welcome addition.

MAKES ABOUT 2½ CUPS (600 ML)

INGREDIENTS

1¼ cups (300 ml) full-bodied red wine or port

⅔ cup (160 ml) water

1 tablespoon sugar

Zest of 1 lemon, removed in strips

¼ teaspoon ground cinnamon

5 egg yolks

In a heavy saucepan, combine the wine, water, sugar, lemon zest, and cinnamon and bring to a boil over high heat. Reduce the heat to a simmer and simmer for 5 minutes. Remove from the heat.

In a bowl, whisk the egg yolks until light and pale yellow. Add the hot liquid a tablespoon or two at a time while whisking constantly. Once about half of the hot liquid has been incorporated, pour in the remaining hot liquid and whisk well.

Pour the mixture back into the saucepan, place over low heat, and bring to a gentle simmer, stirring continuously to prevent curdling, until the sauce thickens and coats the back of a spoon. Immediately remove from the heat and strain through a fine-mesh sieve into a serving bowl. Serve warm.

CUMBERLAND SAUCE

The fruit-based Cumberland sauce was a popular accompaniment to meats in the nineteenth century and appears in *Mrs Beeton's Book of Household Management* and other cookery books of the time. According to Nicolas Soyer, a well-known early twentieth-century British culinary personality, the sauce is perfect with cold venison, so if you have leftovers from the recipe on page 88, it would make a perfect partner. At Sandringham House, the royal estate in Norfolk, the sauce was featured on the sideboard at Christmas dinner in the time of Queen Alexandra, along with beef, brawn, boar's head, chicken, and foie gras.

MAKES ABOUT 1 CUP (250 G)

INGREDIENTS

1 wide orange peel strip

1 wide lemon peel strip

1 teaspoon unsalted butter

1 teaspoon finely chopped shallot

¼ cup (85 g) red currant jelly

1 teaspoon mustard

½ cup (120 ml) red port

Juice of 1 orange

Juice of ½ lemon

Pinch of cayenne pepper

Pinch of ground ginger

Scrape off as much pith as possible from the orange and lemon peel strips, then cut each peel into strips 1⁄16 inch (2 mm) wide or as narrow as you can manage. You'll need about 1 tablespoon of each. Bring a small saucepan of water to a boil over high heat, add the citrus peel strips, and boil for 2 minutes, then drain and let cool.

In a small saucepan, melt the butter over medium-low heat. Add the shallot and cook, stirring, until translucent, about 2 minutes. Do not allow to color. Add the jelly and mustard and stir well, then add the port, orange juice, lemon juice, citrus peel strips, cayenne, and ginger. Bring to a simmer and simmer until the sauce thickens and the flavors blend, about 5 minutes.

Serve warm or cold, depending on your preference.

FOOD FOR THOUGHT

Although he initially considered life as a clergyman, Nicolas Soyer, grandson of the great Victorian chef and philanthropist Alexis Soyer (a relationship disputed by some historians), instead followed in his grandfather's footsteps, becoming a chef and culinary author. He was apprenticed to a confectioner at fifteen and then worked as a chef at many stately homes. Like his grandfather, Nicolas wanted to create a way for people without staff to prepare healthful, well-cooked meals with ease. While Alexis Soyer focused on the poor, Nicolas turned his attention to the middle class, who had either little or no kitchen staff. He was a chef in a new era, the age we witness on *Downton Abbey*, where even the great noble households were having to learn to cope with fewer servants. In 1911, he published the revolutionary Soyer's *Paper-Bag Cookery*, in which he compiled recipes for cooking *en papillote*.

CUSTARD SAUCE

Although the French consider themselves the masters of sauce making, they don't dare take credit for originating custard sauce, calling it *crème anglaise*. They do, however, nearly always flavor their custard sauce with vanilla, as do most British cooks today, which, while quite tasty, can be a bit boring. Older British recipes used a variety of spices, such as bay leaf, cinnamon, mace, and nutmeg, both alone and in combination, to create a more interesting result. If you don't feel adventurous enough to add the mace and bay used here, you can omit them and instead add a few drops of pure vanilla extract to the sauce just as you pour the mixture back into the pan to thicken. This classic sauce complements Christmas Pudding (page 179), Figgy Pudding (page 182), and Christmas Apple Pie (page 191).

MAKES 2½ CUPS (600 ML)

INGREDIENTS

I cup (240 ml) whole milk

I cup (240 ml) heavy cream (preferably at least 40 percent butterfat)

2½ tablespoons Demerara sugar

I blade mace

I fresh bay leaf

5 egg yolks

In a heavy saucepan, combine the milk, cream, sugar, mace, and bay leaf over medium heat and bring just to a gentle simmer, stirring to dissolve the sugar. Remove from the heat.

In a large bowl, whisk the egg yolks until light and pale yellow. Remove and discard the mace and bay from the hot milk mixture. Add the hot liquid a tablespoon or two at a time while whisking constantly. Once about half of the hot liquid has been incorporated, pour in the remaining hot liquid and whisk well. Pour the mixture back into the saucepan, place over low heat, and bring to a gentle simmer, stirring continuously to prevent curdling, until the sauce thickens and coats the back of a spoon.

Remove from the heat and pass through a fine-mesh sieve into a pitcher. Cover with plastic wrap if not serving immediately, pressing it directly onto the surface of the sauce to prevent a skin from forming. Serve warm.

FOOD FOR THOUGHT

Not everything that looks like custard is actually custard. In 1837, Alfred Bird, a chemist living in Birmingham, England, invented imitation custard because his wife was allergic to eggs, a key ingredient of true custard. He came up with a powdered mix that contained cornstarch, salt, color, and flavoring, so the only ingredient the home cook needed to add was milk. Bird's Custard took off, and today many British homes are never without a container of the custard powder in the pantry. Nothing compares to the real thing, of course, but Bird's invention is indeed a quick way to make custard sauce on busy days like Christmas.

PRUNE SAUCE

This recipe appears in *The Cookery Book of Lady Clark of Tillypronie*, a thoughtful survey of Victorian cuisine. Beginning in the 1850s, Lady Clark gathered recipes from hostesses and cooks for nearly five decades, testing them first in the kitchen at Tillypronie before deeming them good enough to be included in the collection.

In this simple sauce, the natural sweetness of the prunes is heightened by the additon of a small amount of sugar, but the subtle sourness inherent in the fruit also comes through, nicely cutting through the richness of the meat the sauce accompanies. During the time of Downton, this sauce would have been served with suckling pig, venison, and mutton. In these pages, it pairs well with the venison on page 88, either alongside the gravy or in place of it; the stuffed mutton leg on page 92; or the mutton chops on page 91.

MAKES 3¼ CUPS (750 ML)

the venison on page 88, either alongside the gravy or in place of it; the stuffed mutton leg on page 92; or the mutton chops on page 91.

INGREDIENTS

I lb (450 g) prunes, pitted	I tablespoon sugar
I¼ cups (300 ml) water	I tablespoon rum or brandy

In a saucepan, combine the prunes and water and bring to a boil over medium-high heat. Adjust the heat to maintain a simmer and cook until the prunes are soft. The timing will depend on how old your prunes are: the older and drier the prunes, the longer they will take to soften.

Add the sugar and simmer until dissolved. Then add the rum, simmer briefly, and remove from the heat. Pass the mixture through a fine-mesh sieve, transfer to a warmed sauceboat, and serve warm. The sauce can also be made a day or two in advance, refrigerated, and gently reheated before serving.

FOOD FOR THOUGHT

In the eighteenth century, the French dubbed the English *les rosbifs*, implying that they ate only roast meat. The great French philosopher and writer Voltaire was equally dismissive of British sauce making, contending that although France's neighbors had seventy religions, they had only one sauce (he failed to cite the name of the sauce). Yet British cookery books have long included numerous sauces, though not of the cream-heavy sort common to French cuisine. Instead, they typically carry sharper, deeper flavors that complement and enhance the meats and other dishes they accompany.

ALFRED

Is this all we're getting? Just these picketty bits?

THOMAS

Hardly. These are canapés, Alfred, for your first course, some truffled egg on toast perhaps? Some oysters à la Russe?

~ SEASON 3, EPISODE 3

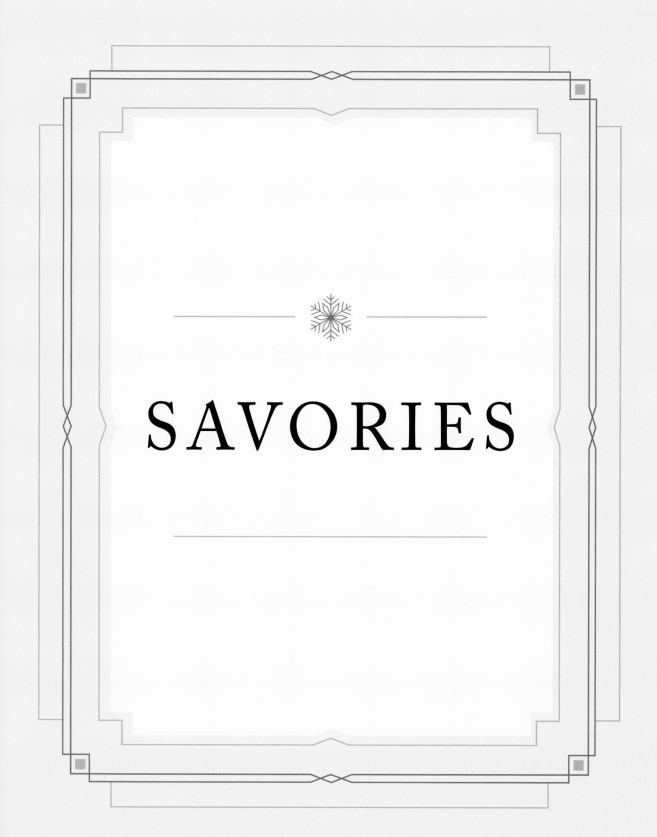

SAVORIES

ANCHOVY ÉCLAIRS

These are among the easiest savories to make. All you need are good-quality puff pastry and a jar of anchovy fillets in oil. Even people who do not like the flavor—or the look—of anchovies will enjoy these little savory puffs. Called éclairs probably because the term sounds elegant, they would make a lovely hors d'oeuvre. But in an Edwardian house at Christmastime, they are more properly served at the end of the meal, after the pudding.

MAKES 12 SMALL PASTRIES; SERVES 6–8

INGREDIENTS

Flour, for the work surface

About 10 oz (285 g) all-butter puff pastry, thawed according to package directions if frozen

12 large or 24 small anchovy fillets in olive oil

1 egg yolk, lightly beaten, for egg wash

Grated Gruyère cheese, for sprinkling

Preheat the oven to 400°F (200°C). Line a sheet pan with parchment paper.

On a lightly floured work surface, roll out the puff pastry a scant ¼ inch (6 mm) thick. Cut out a rectangle about 9 by 8 inches (23 by 20 cm). Cut the rectangle into 12 strips each about 4 by 1½ inches (10 by 4 cm).

With the long side of each strip facing you, place 1 large or 2 small anchovy fillets in the middle of the pastry, leaving ½ inch (12 mm) uncovered on each side. Fold the top of the strip over the fillet(s), enclosing completely, and crimp the edges securely closed with a fork. Brush the top of each pastry with the egg wash and then sprinkle with a little cheese. Carefully transfer the pastries to the prepared pan, spacing them well apart.

Bake the pastries until puffed and golden, 8–10 minutes. Serve hot or at room temperature.

ANGELS ON HORSEBACK

No one is quite sure where this little savory—oysters wrapped in bacon—originated. It was not mentioned in the early editions of *Mrs Beeton's Book of Household Management*, but there is talk of a recipe for *anges à cheval* from Urbain Dubois, who was the chief cook to William I of Prussia beginning in the 1860s. You can make a variation of this dish by replacing the oysters with pitted prunes, which is called devils on horseback.

MAKES 12 OYSTERS; SERVES 6

INGREDIENTS

12 oysters in the shell

6 thin bacon slices, halved crosswise

Woody rosemary sprigs (optional)

Olive oil, for brushing

12 small toast triangles (optional)

Preheat the oven to 375°F (190°C). Line a sheet pan with parchment paper.

To shuck each oyster, protect your nondominant hand with a folded towel and place the oyster, flat side up, on the towel. Locate the hinge in the pointed end, insert the tip of an oyster knife into the hinge, and turn the knife to break the hinge and loosen the shell. Run the blade along the inside surface of the upper shell, detaching the oyster from the shell, and then lift off and discard the top shell. Run the knife along the inside of the rounded bottom shell to detach the oyster, then lift out the oyster and set aside. If using the bottom shells for serving, rinse them and set aside.

Wrap a half bacon slice around an oyster. If you have rosemary in your garden, secure the bacon in place with a small, woody sprig with leaves on top. If you don't have rosemary, secure with a toothpick. Repeat with the remaining oysters and bacon. Arrange the bacon parcels on the prepared pan and brush each parcel with a little oil.

Bake the oysters until the bacon is crisp, 15–20 minutes. Remove from the oven and carefully transfer each parcel to a clean oyster shell or a toast triangle. Serve hot.

PARMESAN BISCUITS

The Cookery Book of Lady Clark of Tillypronie contains hundreds of recipes collected over a lifetime by Charlotte, Lady Clark, who lived at the Victorian-era estate of Tillypronie in Aberdeenshire, Scotland. When Lady Clark died in 1897, her husband, John Forbes Clark, invited family friend Catherine Frances Frere to assemble them into a book. In his letter to Miss Frere, he expresses his strong desire to share his wife's great knowledge of Victorian cookery and extols her many talents.

Clark was a diplomat, which gave Lady Clark the opportunity to live in France, Italy, and Belgium, where she gained insight into European cooking that she later adapted to her own kitchen. British cookery writer Elizabeth David said of Lady Clark's book, "It is for the ideas, the historical aspect and the feeling of authenticity, the certainty that these recipes were actually used and the dishes successful . . . that this book is so valuable." David chose to include this recipe in her book *Spices, Salt and Aromatics in the English Kitchen*. The small, pale-colored biscuits are quite crumbly, and their modest size gives you an excuse to have more than just one!

MAKES ABOUT 30 BISCUITS

INGREDIENTS

¾ cup plus 2 tablespoons (110 g) flour, plus more for the work surface

4 tablespoons (60 g) unsalted butter, cut into cubes

½ cup (60 g) grated Parmesan cheese

1 egg yolk, lightly beaten

Pinch of salt

Pinch of cayenne pepper

Preheat the oven to 325°F (165°C). Line a sheet pan with parchment paper.

Put the flour into a large bowl. Scatter the butter over the flour and, using your fingers, rub the butter into the flour until the mixture forms coarse crumbs. Add the cheese, egg yolk, salt, and cayenne pepper and work them into the flour mixture with a wooden spoon until the dough comes together in a rough mass. Knead in the bowl until smooth and pliable, about 5 minutes.

On a lightly floured work surface, roll out the dough ½ inch (12 mm) thick. Using a 1-inch (2.5-cm) round biscuit cutter, cut out as many rounds as possible. Transfer the rounds to the prepared pan, spacing them about ½ inch (12 mm) apart (the biscuits hold their shape during baking, so they can be closely spaced). Gather up the scraps, reroll them, cut out more rounds, and add them to the pan.

Bake the biscuits until only lightly colored (like pale shortbread), 20–25 minutes. Serve hot.

RECIPE NOTE

Lady Clark says these biscuits should be eaten hot or reheated, though they are just as good, though a bit heavier, when cold.

OYSTERS AU GRATIN

As exquisite as raw oysters are, the prized mollusks were also very popular cooked in the Edwardian era, and a large number of such recipes appear in cookbooks of the time (quite a lot involving Champagne). They were traditionally included in the savory course at the end of the meal, but they were also sometimes offered as hors d'oeuvres. Oysters had once been so plentiful that they were eaten by everyone, and although they were becoming scarcer, and therefore more expensive, by the twentieth century, they were still eaten frequently.

MAKES 24 OYSTERS; SERVES 4

RECIPE NOTE

For a simpler and quicker version of the sauce, use a mixture of 1 teaspoon each sweet chile sauce and heavy cream for each oyster.

INGREDIENTS

½ cup (120 ml) half-and-half

6 tablespoons (90 ml) dry white wine

4 tablespoons (60 g) unsalted butter

1 teaspoon cornstarch

2 anchovy fillets in olive oil, minced

Generous pinch of cayenne pepper

Grated zest of ½ lemon

24 oysters in the shell, scrubbed

⅔ cup (70 g) dried bread crumbs

1 cup (115 g) grated Parmesan cheese

Chopped fresh flat-leaf parsley, for garnish

In a small saucepan, combine the half-and-half, wine, butter, and cornstarch, place over medium heat, and heat, stirring, until the butter melts and all the ingredients are well mixed and heated through. Add the anchovies, cayenne pepper, and lemon zest, stir well, and raise the heat to medium-high. Bring to a gentle boil and boil gently, stirring constantly, until the sauce thickens, about 2 minutes. Remove from the heat and set aside.

To shuck each oyster, protect your nondominant hand with a folded towel and place the oyster, flat side up, on the towel. Locate the hinge in the pointed end, insert the tip of an oyster knife into the hinge, and turn the knife to break the hinge and loosen the shell. Run the blade along the inside surface of the upper shell, detaching the oyster from the shell, and then lift off and discard the top shell. Run the knife along the inside of the rounded bottom shell to detach the oyster, lift out the oyster, and reserve the bottom shell. Rinse all the bottom shells.

Preheat the broiler. In a small bowl, stir together the bread crumbs and Parmesan. Arrange the bottom shells on a large sheet pan. Put a spoonful of the sauce in each bottom shell and lay an oyster on top. Sprinkle the bread crumb mixture evenly over the oysters. Broil until the cheese is bubbling and the topping is crisp, 3–4 minutes. Serve hot, garnished with parsley.

MACARONI AND CHEESE TARTLETS

This is a recipe from Nicolas Soyer, the grandson of the great Victorian chef Alexis Soyer and a well-known figure on the British culinary stage in the early twentieth century. The tartlets are very tasty and filling and are best eaten warm from the oven. When they are allowed to cool, they become quite heavy and dry.

MAKES 24 TARTLETS

INGREDIENTS

FOR THE PASTRY

1¾ cups (225 g) flour, plus more for the work surface

½ cup (60 g) grated Parmesan cheese

Pinch of salt

Pinch of cayenne pepper

4 tablespoons (60 g) cold unsalted butter, cut into cubes

1 egg, lightly beaten

5 tablespons (75 ml) ice-cold water

FOR THE FILLING

2 oz (60 g) very small dried macaroni (about ½ cup)

½ cup (60 g) grated Parmesan or Gruyère cheese

6½ tablespoons (100 ml) heavy cream

Small pinch of salt

Small pinch of cayenne pepper

Chopped fresh flat-leaf parsley, for garnish (optional)

To make the pastry, in a bowl, stir together the flour, cheese, salt, and cayenne pepper. Scatter the butter over the flour mixture and, using your fingers, work in the butter until the mixture is the consistency of bread crumbs. Pour in the egg and then gradually add the water, stirring and tossing with a fork just until the mixture comes together in a rough mass. Transfer the dough to a work surface, pat into a smooth ball, and flatten into a disk. Wrap in plastic wrap and refrigerate for 30 minutes.

Preheat the oven to 350°F (180°C). Have ready two 12-well tartlet pans with wells about 2½ inches (6 cm) in diameter at the top and ½ inch (12 mm) deep.

On a lightly floured work surface, roll out the pastry ⅟₁₆ inch (2 mm) thick or as thinly as possible. Using a 3-inch (7.5-cm) round pastry cutter, cut out as many rounds as possible. Transfer the pastry rounds to the tartlet wells, pressing them onto the bottom and up the sides. If needed, gather up the pastry scraps and reroll them to make enough rounds to fill all the wells. Prick the pastry all over with a fork. Cut out rounds of parchment paper a bit larger than the tartlet wells, crumple them up and flatten again, and then slip a parchment round into each pastry-lined well. Add a few pie weights or a teaspoon or so of raw rice to each well.

Recipe continues

Bake the tartlet shells until lightly golden, about 20 minutes. The pastry will not color much. Remove the pans from the oven, remove the pie weights and parchment, and return the pans to the oven until the pastry is fully dry, 3–4 minutes. Let cool in the pans on wire racks. Leave the oven on and position an oven rack in the upper third of the oven.

To make the filling, bring a saucepan of salted water to a boil, add the macaroni, and cook until just shy of al dente, according to the package directions. Meanwhile, put the cheese into a bowl. When the macaroni is ready, drain it, add it to the bowl with the cheese, and stir together. (If you have been unable to find very small macaroni, chop the cooked macaroni before adding it to the cheese.) Now, bring the cream to a simmer in a small saucepan over medium heat, add the salt and cayenne pepper, pour over the macaroni and cheese, and stir to bind the mixture.

Spoon the filling into the tartlet shells, dividing it evenly, and slip the pans onto the top rack of the oven. Bake until the filling is slightly golden, 15–20 minutes. Remove from the oven, let sit for a minute or two, and then use the tip of a small knife to ease the tartlets out of the pans. Garnish with parsley, if using, and serve warm.

RECIPE NOTE

If you prefer to make only 12 tartlets, cut the ingredient amounts for the filling in half and then make the filling as directed. Make the pastry dough as directed, then cut the dough in half and use half for making the 12 tartlets. Wrap the remaining half in plastic wrap and refrigerate for up to 3 days, or slip the wrapped dough into a zip-lock bag and freeze for up to 1 month. Use it for making another batch of these tartlets or for making the Shrimp Tartlets à la Diable on page 173.

ON SAVORIES

Small, brightly flavored bites, savories were traditionally served at the end of a formal multicourse meal, after the entremets (sweets) and alongside fresh fruits and ices. But savories could also be snacks or even lunch, as we see on Christmas Day at Downton Abbey in season 2, episode 9. The servants have arranged an array of savories on the sideboard for the Crawley family, who will be helping themselves to them while the staff enjoys their holiday feast downstairs. This Christmas self-serve lunch would have been a rare occurrence in noble houses of the time, where servants had to bend to the needs of the family, rather than the family showing any accommodation toward the staff.

Designed to be palate cleansers, savories were usually salty, creamy, or spicy and could typically be eaten in one or two bites, often without the need for cutlery. In her 1922 book *Kitchen Essays*, Lady Agnes Jekyll writes that these petite, delicious morsels also provided an option for people who, for any reason, were abstaining from eating sweets. In some cases, gentlemen might pass on the sweets and instead eat a couple of savories and then excuse themselves so they might enjoy a whisky together in another room. The ladies often sampled the sweets and then left the table to sip sherry and chat elsewhere.

Multicourse meals were becoming less common by the early 1920s. Aristocratic families of the time found themselves having to economize to save their grand estates, which meant, among other efforts, scaling down formal meals and employing fewer servants, a trend we see happening at Downton. At the same time, some people were questioning the need for the strict dinner etiquette of the past. Not surprisingly, the Dowager Countess is openly resistant to changing the formalities surrounding mealtime, but we see other family members showing a preference for a less complicated protocol.

Although herself a very modern woman, Jekyll comments that an evening without the option of sweet and savory would be a little disappointing. She mentions cheese on toast, or Welsh rarebit, and roasted marrowbones with toast, but she also describes more elegant—and more fitting for a home like Downton—dishes, such as gratineed oysters on a scallop shell, dainty puff pastry boats filled with all manner of foods, and caviar, foie gras, and thin slices of smoked salmon with a choice of brown or white bread. Mushrooms, she offers, are also useful for the savories repertoire.

The custom of serving a savories course continued in Britain until the mid-twentieth century, though now it has largely disappeared. Today, many of the same bites can be eaten as hors d'oeuvres with an aperitif, a good way to include these classic offerings in a Downton-inspired dinner.

SHRIMP TARTLETS À LA DIABLE

Diable in a recipe title means the food is "deviled," or flavored with a hot, spicy, or sharp seasoning. Here, both the pastry and the filling include cayenne pepper, but other recipes might use curry powder, mustard, or Worcestershire sauce. Deviled foods first became common in the eighteenth century and remain popular today.

This recipe appeared in the 1906 edition of *A Book of Salads* by Alfred Suzanne. The author stretches the definition of salads to include both meat-heavy platters with just a few leaves of lettuce and these scrumptious little tarts. At Downton Abbey, the tartlets might be served as a savory after the pudding for Christmas dinner, set out on the sideboard for Christmas lunch, or offered as an hor d'oeuvre at a holiday party.

MAKES 12 TARTLETS

INGREDIENTS

FOR THE PASTRY

1¾ cups (225 g) flour, plus more for the work surface

½ cup (60 g) grated Parmesan cheese

Pinch of salt

Pinch of cayenne pepper

4 tablespoons (60 g) cold unsalted butter, cut into cubes

1 egg, lightly beaten

5 tablespons (75 ml) ice-cold water

FOR THE FILLING

½ lb (225 g) cooked and peeled small shrimp (see Recipe Note, page 174)

2 tablespoons mayonnaise

¼ teaspoon cayenne pepper

Chopped fresh tarragon or flat-leaf parsley, for garnish

Cayenne pepper, for dusting

To make the pastry, in a bowl, stir together the flour, cheese, salt, and cayenne pepper. Scatter the butter over the flour mixture and, using your fingers, work in the butter until the mixture is the consistency of bread crumbs. Pour in the egg and then gradually add the water, stirring and tossing with a fork just until the mixture comes together in a rough mass. Transfer the dough to a work surface, pat into a smooth ball, and cut in half. Flatten each half into a disk. Wrap 1 disk in plastic wrap and refrigerate for 30 minutes. Wrap the second disk in plastic wrap and refrigerate for up to 3 days, or slip the wrapped dough into a zip-lock bag and freeze for up to 1 month.

Preheat the oven to 350°F (180°C). Have ready one 12-well tartlet pan with wells about 2½ inches (6 cm) in diameter at the top and ½ inch (12 mm) deep.

On a lightly floured work surface, roll out the pastry ¹⁄₁₆ inch (2 mm) thick or as thinly as possible. Using a 3-inch (7.5-cm) round pastry cutter, cut out as many rounds as possible. Transfer the pastry rounds to the tartlet wells, pressing them onto the bottom and up the sides. If needed, gather up the pastry scraps and reroll them to make enough rounds to fill all the wells. Prick the pastry all over with a fork. Cut out rounds of parchment paper a bit larger than the tartlet wells, crumple them up and flatten again, and then slip a parchment round into each pastry-lined well. Add a few pie weights or a teaspoon or so of raw rice to each well.

Recipe continues

Bake the tartlet shells until lightly golden, about 20 minutes. The pastry will not color much. Remove the pan from the oven, remove the pie weights and parchment, and return the pan to the oven until the pastry is fully dry, 3–4 minutes. Let cool completely in the pan on a wire rack while you assemble the filling.

To make the filling, combine the shrimp, mayonnaise, and cayenne pepper in a bowl and stir together gently, mixing well.

Using the tip of a small knife, ease the cooled tartlet shells out of the pan. Spoon the filling into the shells, dividing it evenly. Garnish the filling with tarragon and a light dusting of cayenne pepper. Arrange on a platter or tray and serve.

RECIPE NOTE

Small shrimp, such as bay, salad shrimp, or prawns, work best in these tiny tarts. Use whatever you can find locally.

ATTICUS: *She wouldn't know if it was Christmas or Tuesday.*

ROSE: *What a man thing to say.*

ATTICUS: *She's only three months old.*

ROSE: *But such a clever three months!*

~ SEASON 6, EPISODE 9

MRS. PATMORE

Fold it in, don't slap it! You're making a cake, not beating a carpet!

~ SEASON 2, EPISODE 2

DESSERTS
& SWEETS

CHRISTMAS PUDDING

At Downton, a Christmas pudding would have been served as dessert for the holiday dinner, as is done today. Traditionally, this iconic dish was called plum pudding (the word *plum* was understood as any dried fruit) and was a common companion to roast beef on festive days.

The first recorded recipe of plum pudding similar to what is made today is found in John Nott's *The Cook's and Confectioner's Dictionary*, published in 1723. But the first time the pudding was associated specifically with Christmas appears in 1649 in the diary of Colonel Henry Norwood, who was on board a ship that had set sail for London from Virginia in September. Although the ship went off course in stormy seas and was almost out of food, a plum pudding made from what little remained in its stores was served on Christmas.

This recipe is adapted from one included in Dorothy Allhusen's *A Book of Scents and Other Dishes*. It comes from Mrs. Thomas Hardy, the second wife of the famed novelist and poet, and had been in his family for generations. Interestingly, Thomas Hardy was known to dislike Christmas pudding.

SERVES 6–8

INGREDIENTS

1 cup (150 g) dark raisins

1 cup (150 g) dried currants

½ cup (75 g) golden raisins

5¼ oz (150 g) shredded suet (about 1¼ cups)

2¾ cups (110 g) fresh bread crumbs

⅓ cup (40 g) flour

2 tablespoons natural almonds, finely chopped

1 teaspoon mixed spice

½ teaspoon ground nutmeg

½ teaspoon salt

1 egg, lightly beaten

2½ tablespoons whole milk

2½ tablespoons dark rum

2½ tablespoons brandy

3 tablespoons stout or other dark beer

Grated zest and juice of ½ lemon

Unsalted butter, for the mold

Boiling water, for steaming

Custard Sauce (page 155), for serving

Brandy or rum, for drizzling

Start the pudding a day ahead of steaming so the mixture can rest. In a large bowl, combine the dark raisins, currants, golden raisins, suet, bread crumbs, flour, almonds, mixed spice, nutmeg, and salt and mix well with a wooden spoon. Add the egg, milk, rum, brandy, stout, and lemon zest and juice and stir gently until all the ingredients are evenly distributed. Cover the bowl and refrigerate overnight.

Preheat the oven to 325°F (165°C). Generously butter a 5-cup (1.2-l) pudding mold. Cut a round of parchment paper to fit the bottom of the mold, then press it against the bottom so it sticks to the butter. When the pudding is ready to serve, the parchment will make it easier to unmold it.

Transfer the pudding mixture to the prepared mold, packing it firmly. Cut out a round of parchment 3–4 inches (7.5–10 cm) larger than the diameter of the top of the mold. Make a narrow fold across the center of the round so the paper can expand as the pudding rises during cooking, then lay the parchment on top of the pudding. Fold down the overhang and secure the parchment in place with kitchen string. Cover the parchment with aluminum foil or a kitchen towel. Tie kitchen string around the rim to secure the towel or foil, making a little handle on either side of the mold to use for lifting the mold out of the pot after cooking.

Recipe continues

Select a heavy ovenproof pot large enough to hold the pudding mold with room for circulating steam. Place an inverted ovenproof saucer, a canning jar ring, or a trivet on the bottom of the pot and set the mold on it. Pour boiling water into the pot to come halfway up the sides of the mold. Cover the pot with its lid or aluminum foil and transfer it to the oven.

Steam the pudding for 3–4 hours, checking the water level once every hour and adding more boiling water as needed to maintain the original level. To check if the pudding is done, remove the pot from the oven and, using the string handles, carefully lift out the pudding mold. Open the coverings and press the top of the pudding with a fingertip. If it springs back, the pudding is done. If it leaves a depression, rewrap the pudding, return it to the pot and then to the oven, and steam for 1 hour longer.

When the pudding is ready, again using the string handles, lift the mold from the pot. Snip the string and remove the coverings. If you will be serving it right away, invert a serving plate on top of the mold, then invert the mold and plate together, lift off the mold, and peel off the parchment. Slice and serve warm with the Custard Sauce in a sauceboat alongside.

This pudding, like fruitcake, is best if made in advance of serving. This allows the flavors to mature and gives you the opportunity to add additional brandy or rum, which helps to both flavor and preserve the pudding. Let the pudding cool in the uncovered mold, top with fresh parchment paper, and secure the paper in place with kitchen string. Store the pudding in a cool cupboard for up to 3 months and feed it with a couple of teaspoons of brandy once a week. When it is time to serve it, re-cover the mold with parchment and a towel or foil and steam it in the oven the same way until heated through, about 1 hour. Or to reheat in a microwave, remove the parchment, place the mold directly in the microwave, and microwave just until hot and steamy, which should take just a few minutes but no longer than 10 minutes.

RECIPE NOTE

Serving the pudding with a custard sauce is not the only option. It is also good with Brandy Butter (page 151) or brandy sauce, ice cream, or clotted or heavy cream. Although not at all traditional, it also pairs well with a wedge of blue cheese.

A great deal of steam! The pudding was out of the copper. A smell like a washing-day! That was the cloth. A smell like an eating-house and a pastrycook's next door to each other, with a laundress's next door to that! That was the pudding! In half a minute Mrs. Cratchit entered—flushed, but smiling proudly—with the pudding, like a speckled cannon-ball, so hard and firm, blazing in half of half-a-quartern of ignited brandy, and bedight with Christmas holly stuck into the top.

—CHARLES DICKENS, *A CHRISTMAS CAROL*, 1843

ON PLUM PUDDING

Eating beef and plum pudding on special occasions had become so emblematic of British custom by the early nineteenth century that it was considered an act of patriotism during the Napoleonic Wars. That patriotic sentiment continued into World War I, when Lady Rawlinson, wife of Sir Henry Rawlinson, a much-decorated British Army officer, gifted a Christmas pudding to each man in her husband's corps. In the same period, British women working in refugee camps in France and Belgium contributed to the national spirit by embroidering patriotic themes onto postcards. Among the most sought-after image was a plum pudding bristling with flags.

But the patriotism surrounding the plum pudding continued even beyond the war years. In 1925, Australian fruit growers paraded through the streets of London carrying a huge Christmas pudding outfitted with a sign announcing, "Make your pudding of Empire products." Just two years later, George V made the campaign his own by encouraging the people to use ingredients sourced from the British Empire, rather than cheap imports from America, for their Christmas pudding. His chef, Mr. Cédard, provided the Empire Marketing Board with the palace's Empire Christmas pudding recipe, which included the source of each ingredient, from Canadian flour to South African raisins. To follow the recipe was to show loyalty to king and country.

As dining fashions changed near the end of the nineteenth century, and sweet dishes moved toward the end of the meal, the plum pudding migrated along with them. It also went from being round and boiled in a cloth to steamed in a decorative mold. Even though it seems illogical to have such a filling pudding after starters, side dishes, and so much meat, by the Downton era, the Christmas pudding marked the end of the meal. And when in season 2, episode 9, it is carried into the room by Carson, it is clear that this is where the family has always seen the plum pudding and where it will forever remain. Christmas is all about tradition, and not having Christmas pudding on Christmas Eve might feel like you could be jinxing the New Year.

FIGGY PUDDING

Just as the "plum" in plum pudding refers to raisins or currants (before Victorian days, the word *plum* was used for any dried fruit), the "figgy" in figgy pudding refers to raisins or currants. But that is not all these two puddings share. Figgy pudding is actually just another name for plum pudding, a British Christmas-table staple. Some ascribe the coining to the fact that the speckled flesh of the fig resembles the speckled look of plum pudding. But in time, people did start to make this pudding with figs rather than only raisins or currants. The result is a pudding that looks Moorish in inspiration and as if it is bedecked with dark burgundy garnets—a dessert fit for a grand Christmas feast!

SERVES 4–6

INGREDIENTS

14 oz (400 g) dried figs

3 tablespoons golden syrup

½ cup (120 ml) fruity red wine or red port

4 teaspoons Cointreau

6½ tablespoons (60 g) dried currants

FOR THE PUDDING

Unsalted butter, for the mold

¾ cup plus 2 tablespoons (110 g) flour

½ cup (120 g) firmly packed dark brown sugar

1½ cups (60 g) fresh bread crumbs

2 oz (60 g) shredded suet (about ½ cup)

1 teaspoon baking powder

1 teaspoon mixed spice

½ teaspoon ground nutmeg

Pinch of salt

2 eggs, lightly beaten

5 tablespoons (75 ml) stout or other dark beer

Boiling water, for steaming

Custard Sauce (page 155) or clotted cream, for serving

Start the pudding a day ahead of steaming. In a saucepan, combine the figs, golden syrup, wine, and Cointreau and bring to a simmer over medium heat. Simmer, stirring to keep the figs immersed in the liquid, until softened, about 5 minutes. Using a slotted spoon, transfer the figs to a plate. Continue to simmer the liquid until it becomes syrupy, about 10 minutes. Meanwhile, cut off any tough stems from the figs, then halve the figs lengthwise. When the syrup is ready, pour it into a heatproof bowl, add the figs, and let soak at room temperature overnight. In a small bowl, combine the currants with water to cover and let soak at room temperature overnight.

The next day, preheat the oven to 325°F (165°C). Generously butter a 5-cup (1.2-l) pudding mold. Cut a round of parchment paper to fit the bottom of the mold, then press it against the bottom so it sticks to the butter. When the pudding is ready to serve, the parchment will make it easier to unmold it.

To make the pudding, in a large bowl, combine the flour, sugar, bread crumbs, suet, baking powder, mixed spice, nutmeg, and salt and mix well with a wooden spoon. Drain the currants, add to the bowl along with the eggs and stout, and mix well.

Remove the figs from the syrup and arrange them, cut side down, on the bottom and sides of the mold, covering the surface completely. They will stick to the sides because of the syrup. Cut up any remaining figs and fold them into tthe pudding mixture. Reserve the syrup for serving.

Spoon the pudding mixture into the prepared mold, packing it firmly while being careful not to dislodge the figs on the bottom and sides. Cut out a round of parchment 3–4 inches (7.5–10 cm) larger than the diameter of the top of the mold. Make a narrow fold across the center of the round so the paper can expand as the pudding rises during cooking, then lay the parchment on top of the pudding. Fold down the overhang and secure the parchment in place with kitchen string. Cover the parchment with aluminum foil or a kitchen towel, again making a narrow fold across the center to allow room for the pudding to rise as it cooks. Tie kitchen string around the rim to secure the towel or foil, making a little handle on either side of the mold to use for lifting the mold out of the pot after cooking.

Select a heavy ovenproof pot large enough to hold the pudding mold with room for circulating steam. Place an inverted ovenproof saucer, a canning jar ring, or a trivet on the bottom of the pot and set the mold on it. Pour boiling water into the pot to come halfway up the sides of the mold. Cover the pot with its lid or aluminum foil and transfer it to the oven.

Steam the pudding for 3 hours, checking the water level once every hour and adding more boiling water as needed to maintain the original level.

When the pudding is ready, using the string handles, carefully lift the mold from the pot. Snip the string and remove the coverings. Invert a serving plate on top of the mold, then invert the mold and plate together, lift off the mold, and peel off the parchment. Warm any leftover syrup and drizzle over the pudding. Slice and serve warm with the Custard Sauce alongside.

Carson carries in the pudding.

EDITH: *Sybil's favourite.*

Carson brings it to Violet's left. She holds a spoon up.

VIOLET: *A happy Christmas to us all.*

She plunges the spoon in.

ALL: *Happy Christmas.*

~ SEASON 2, EPISODE 9

CHESTNUT PUDDINGS

This recipe comes from *Recherché Luncheon and Dinner Sweets*, published in 1906 and written by Charles Herman Senn, a noted food authority of the late nineteenth and early twentieth century. Senn published a number of cookery books, with his wartime works among his best known. Although he was highly regarded in his time, little is known about him today.

Chestnuts are a seasonal favorite, and as they are not used much in sweet desserts today, the flavor of these puddings may surprise your guests. Mrs. Patmore would have had to instruct one of her kitchen maids to cook and peel the chestnuts for this recipe, a tedious task. Fortunately nowadays, they are sold cooked and peeled and the quality is excellent.

SERVES 6–8

RECIPE NOTE
Plastic lidded pudding molds are ideal for steaming these little puddings, but any custard cups or small heatproof bowls will work with aluminum foil for the cover.

INGREDIENTS

½ cup (115 g) unsalted butter, at room temperature, plus more for the molds

3 oz (90 g) jarred or vacuum-packed roasted and peeled whole chestnuts, plus 6 chestnuts

¼ cup (60 g) firmly packed light brown sugar

2 eggs

3½ tablespoons (65 g) golden syrup

2 cups (80 g) fresh bread crumbs

4 teaspoons kirsch or brandy

¾ cup plus 1 tablespoon (115 g) flour

18–24 whole blanched almonds

Boiling water, for steaming

Preheat the oven to 350°F (180°C). Butter six–eight 5–fl oz (150-ml) pudding molds or other heatproof bowls. Cut a round of parchment paper to fit the bottom of each mold, then press a round onto the bottom of each mold so it sticks to the butter.

Pass the 3 oz (90 g) chestnuts through a coarse-mesh sieve and reserve. In a bowl, using a wooden spoon, beat together the butter and sugar until smooth and creamy. Add the eggs one at a time, beating well after each addition. Add the golden syrup and mix well. Stir in the grated chestnuts and then the bread crumbs and kirsch. Finally, fold in the flour until fully incorporated.

Break the 6 whole chestnuts into appealing-size pieces. Place a large piece of chestnut in the center of the bottom of each prepared mold and arrange 3 almonds around it. Scoop the batter on top, dividing it evenly among the molds. Divide the remaining chestnut pieces evenly among the molds, pressing them into the batter.

Wrap each pudding basin with aluminum foil, or pop on the lid if you are using plastic pudding basins (see Recipe Note). Place all the puddings in a large, deep baking pan and pour boiling water into the pan to come halfway up the sides of the molds. Cover the pan with foil, pressing it firmly against the sides, then cover the foil with a kitchen towel and secure in place with kitchen string.

Steam the puddings in the oven until a toothpick inserted into the center of a pudding comes out clean, 40–50 minutes. Remove from the oven and, one at a time, uncover the puddings, invert onto individual plates or a tray, and peel off the parchment. Serve warm.

WARTIME CHRISTMAS PUDDING

During World War I, sugar, flour, and eggs were hard to come by, so cooks—Mrs. Patmore and regular housewives—had to come up with creative ways to serve a treat, especially for Christmas. Potato and carrot often stood in for more costly ingredients, as they were plentiful and heavily promoted by the Ministry of Food. They both appear in this recipe, which is taken from a Ministry of Food war cookery leaflet, where it was titled War & Peace Pudding. It is an excellent example of the very English custom of making do without letting go of tradition. After all, it's not Christmas without a proper pudding!

There is no sugar in this recipe, as sugar was particularly dear, but if the pudding is eaten with jam, you likely won't miss the sweetness. However, because a bit of sugar does improve the flavor, the option to add it has been included. The potato is indiscernible, but the taste of the carrot, in combination with the spice, comes through beautifully. If you like carrot cake, this is for you.

SERVES 4–6

INGREDIENTS

Unsalted butter, for the mold

1 cup (100 g) grated potato

⅔ cup (75 g) grated carrot

⅔ cup (85 g) flour

⅔ cup (30 g) fresh bread crumbs

1 oz (30 g) shredded suet (about ¼ cup)

2½ tablespoons sugar (optional)

1 teaspoon ground allspice, mixed spice, or ground cinnamon

1 teaspoon baking soda

2 tablespoons warm water

¼ cup (30 g) mixed dried fruits (such as currants, raisins, and chopped citrus peel), soaked in water, rum, or brandy until plumped, then drained

Boiling water, for steaming

Preheat the oven to 325°F (165°C). Generously butter a 2½-cup (600-ml) pudding mold. Cut a round of parchment paper to fit the bottom of the mold, then press it against the bottom so it sticks to the butter. When the pudding is ready to serve, the parchment will make it easier to unmold it.

In a medium bowl, combine the potato, carrot, flour, bread crumbs, suet, sugar (if using), and allspice. In a small bowl, dissolve the baking soda in the water, add to the potato mixture, and stir with a wooden spoon until the ingredients are evenly distributed and a shaggy dough forms.

Lightly flour a work surface, turn the dough out onto it, and knead until it comes together in a smooth ball. Don't be alarmed if the mixture seems dry; it will come together after kneading for only a few minutes. Flatten the dough slightly, scatter the dried fruits over it, and then gently work them into the dough, distributing them evenly. Shape the dough into a ball.

Transfer the dough to the prepared mold and press down firmly. Cut out a round of parchment 3–4 inches (7.5–10 cm) larger than the diameter of the top of the mold. Make a narrow fold across the center of the round so the paper can expand as the pudding rises during cooking, then lay the parchment on top of the pudding. Fold down the overhang and secure the parchment in place with kitchen string. Cover the parchment with aluminum foil or a kitchen towel, again making a narrow fold across the center to allow room for the pudding to rise as it cooks. Tie kitchen string around the rim to secure the towel or foil, making a little handle on either side of the mold to use for lifting the mold out of the pot after cooking.

Select a heavy ovenproof pot large enough to hold the pudding mold with room for circulating steam. Place an inverted ovenproof saucer, a canning jar ring, or a trivet on the bottom of the pot and set the mold on it. Pour boiling water into the pot to come halfway up the sides of the mold. Cover the pot with its lid or aluminum foil and transfer it to the oven.

Steam the pudding for 2 hours, checking the water level after the first hour and adding more boiling water as needed to maintain the original level.

When the pudding is ready, using the string handles, carefully lift the mold from the pot. Snip the string and remove the coverings. Invert a serving plate on top of the mold, then invert the mold and plate together, lift off the mold, and peel off the parchment. Slice and serve warm.

MRS. PATMORE: *Now hold it right there! If we can't feed a few soldiers in our own village, them as've taken a bullet or worse for King and Country, then I don't know what!*

~ SEASON 2, EPISODE 4

MINCE PIES

Mince pie was on the table of the nobility in medieval times. The filling mixed fruits, spices, brandy, suet, and meat (or sometimes even fish), with beef, veal, or ox tongue the most common choices. The pie made an appearance at every major special occasion but was increasingly favored at Christmas. Then, with the arrival of Puritan rule in 1640s, mince pies were banished along with other festive foods, returning to the table in 1660 with the restoration of the monarchy. By this time, the large pies of the Middle Ages had been replaced by smaller ones in a variety of shapes.

During the nineteenth century, the pies were made with shortcrust or puff pastry or with a mix: the base was shortcrust and the top was puff pastry. *Mrs Beeton's Book of Household Management* gives recipes for mincemeat with and without meat. By the twentieth century, however, the filling no longer included meat, and the pies were a firmly established Christmas tradition. Mrs. Patmore would have learned to make them the Victorian way, however, with just enough meat to provide a subtle note of flavor. Both options are included here in this recipe adapted from Mrs. Beeton's.

MAKES 18 SMALL PIES

INGREDIENTS

FOR THE MINCEMEAT

1 lemon

1 cooking apple, cored, peeled, and chopped

1 teaspoon unsalted butter

1½ cups (300 g) firmly packed dark brown sugar

5¼ oz (150 g) shredded suet (about 1¼ cups)

1 cup (150 g) raisins

1 cup (150 g) dried currants

1 oz (30 g) candied citrus peel, finely chopped

5 tablespoons (75 ml) brandy

2 teaspoons orange marmalade

FOR THE PASTRY

2¾ cups (345 g) flour, plus more for the work surface and the pans

⅓ cup (40 g) confectioners' sugar

Pinch of sea salt

¾ cup plus 2 tablespoons (200 g) cold butter, cut into cubes, plus room-temperature butter for the pans

2 tablespoons ice-cold water

2 egg yolks, lightly beaten

FOR THE SWEET FILLING

14 oz (400 g) mincemeat (about 1¾ cups)

FOR THE SWEET FILLING WITH MEAT

¾ lb (340 g) mincemeat (about 1½ cups)

Unsalted butter, for frying

2 oz (60 g) coarsely ground or finely chopped lamb or mutton

1 egg yolk beaten with 1 tablespoon whole milk, for egg wash

To make the mincemeat, grate the zest from the lemon into a small bowl. Halve the lemon and squeeze the juice into the bowl with the zest. In a small saucepan, combine the lemon flesh with water to cover, bring to a boil over medium-high heat, and boil until tender, 5–7 minutes. At the same time, in a second small saucepan, combine the apple and butter over medium heat and stew the apple, stirring occasionally, until soft, about 8 minutes. Remove the lemon and apple from the heat and let cool.

Finely chop together the cooked apple and lemon flesh until reduced to a pulp. Scoop into a bowl, add the lemon zest and juice, sugar, suet, raisins, currants, citrus peel, brandy, and marmalade and mix well. You should have about 30 oz (880 g). Spoon the mincemeat into sterilized jars (two 1-pint/475-ml jars should hold it), cap, and, if possible, refrigerate for 10 days before using. It will mature in flavor as it sits.

Recipe continues

To make the pastry, in a large bowl, whisk together the flour, sugar, and salt. Scatter the butter over the top and, using your fingers, rub in the butter until the mixture is the consistency of bread crumbs. Add the water and egg yolks and mix with a fork until the mixture forms a rough mass. Knead on a lightly floured surface just until the dough is smooth, then pat into a ball, wrap in plastic wrap, and refrigerate for 30 minutes.

While the pastry rests, ready the filling. If using the sweet filling, use the mincemeat straight from the jar. If using the sweet filling with meat, scoop the mincemeat into a bowl. In a small frying pan, melt a little butter over medium heat, add the lamb, and cook, stirring, just until cooked, 5–8 minutes. Do not allow to brown. Let cool, then add to the mincemeat and mix well.

Preheat the oven to 350°F (180°C). Using two 12-well tartlet pans with wells about 2½ inches (6 cm) in diameter at the top and ½ inch (12 mm) deep, butter 18 wells. Dust lightly with flour.

Cut off one-third of the pastry, rewrap the smaller piece, and refrigerate. On a lightly floured surface, roll out the remaining dough about ⅛ inch (3 mm) thick. Using a 3-inch (7.5-cm) round pastry cutter, cut out as many rounds as possible. Transfer the rounds to the prepared tartlet wells, pressing them onto the bottom and up the sides. Gather up the pastry scraps, reroll, and cut out more rounds as needed to fill 18 wells total. Prick the bottom of each pastry shell three times with a fork.

To make lids for the pies, roll out the remaining dough about ⅛ inch (3 mm) thick. Choose a cutter in the shape you like and about 2½ inches (6 cm) in diameter. Stars are traditional, though Mrs. Patmore would have probably used rounds. Cut out the lids, rerolling the scraps as needed to make 18 lids.

Divide the filling evenly among the pastry shells and press down gently. Top with the lids. If using stars or another shape, no need to crimp. If using rounds, cut a small hole in the center, then crimp the lid to the rim. Brush the lids and rim with the egg wash.

Bake the pies until the pastry is golden brown, 20–25 minutes. Let cool in the pans on wire racks for at least 5 minutes, then serve warm or at room temperature. Use the tip of a small knife to ease the pies out of the pans.

BERTIE: *Are you pining for some unfulfilled dream?*

EDITH: *Not today. Today I feel very happy.*

~ SEASON 5, EPISODE 9

CHRISTMAS APPLE PIE

A Christmas apple pie was included in Florence White's *Good Things in England*, published in 1932. In her introduction to the recipe, which dates to the eighteenth century, she says it was traditional in and around Potton, Bedfordshire, to place a large apple pie on the table for the Christmas festivities. Called an apple florentine, it was made on a pewter or sometimes silver plate and was filled with "good baking apples." The pie had only a top crust, or lid, and to serve it, the pastry was lifted off, cut into triangular pieces, spiced ale was poured over the apples, and the lid was returned to the top. Then everyone was served a portion each of apple and crust.

The custom of removing a pie lid is centuries old. It was even popular to lift off the lid and replace it with a more elaborately fashioned top for serving. The fancy crust was often purely decorative and saved and used again on the next special occasion. This recipe honors White's holiday apple pie, but it is made with a double crust, in the manner of the Edwardian times.

SERVES 6–8

INGREDIENTS

FOR THE SHORTCRUST PASTRY

2 cups (250 g) flour, plus more for the dish and the work surface

¾ cup plus 2 tablespoons (100 g) confectioners' sugar

Pinch of sea salt

½ cup plus 2 teaspoons (125 g) cold unsalted butter, cut into cubes, plus room-temperature butter for the dish

1 egg, lightly beaten

1 tablespoon water

1¾ lb (800 g) cooking apples, peeled, cored, and cut into ¾-inch (2-cm) dice

½ cup (100 g) Demerara sugar

Grated zest of 1 lemon

1 egg yolk beaten with 1 tablespoon whole milk, for egg wash

3½ tablespoons (50 g) unsalted butter, cut into small cubes

Vanilla ice cream, clotted cream, or Custard Sauce (page 155), for serving

To make the pastry, in a food processor, combine the flour, confectioners' sugar, and salt and process briefly to mix well. Scatter the butter over the flour mixture and pulse until the mixture resembles coarse bread crumbs, about 8 seconds. Add the egg and water and pulse again just until the dough comes together in a rough ball. Transfer the dough to a work surface and knead briefly to bring it together. Do not overwork the dough or it will be tough. Cut the dough in half, flatten each half into a thick disk, wrap in plastic wrap, and refrigerate for 30 minutes.

Preheat the oven to 375°F (190°C). Butter a 9-inch (23-cm) pie dish, then dust with flour, tapping out the excess.

In a large bowl, toss the apples with the Demerara sugar and lemon zest, coating the apples evenly.

On a lightly floured work surface, roll out half the pastry into a round about 12 inches (30 cm) in diameter and ½ inch (12 mm) thick. Roll the dough around the pin, center the pin over the prepared pie dish, and unroll the dough, centering it in the dish and allowing the excess to overhang the sides. Gently press the dough onto the bottom and up the sides of the dish. Trim off the excess pastry, leaving a ¾-inch (2-cm) overhang. Brush the rim of the pastry with the egg wash.

Recipe continues

Spoon the apple filling into the pie dish and dot the top with the butter cubes. Roll out the remaining pastry into a round the same way and carefully slide it over the filling, making sure to center it. Trim any excess to a ¾-inch (2-cm) overhang, then press the top crust against the bottom crust to seal, fold under the edges, and crimp with a fork or flute with your fingers. Using a paring knife, cut a cross or a small hole in the center of the top crust to allow steam to escape while the pie is baking. If you like, use any pastry scraps for making decorations: Press together the scraps, roll out about ½ inch (12 mm) thick, and cut out leaves or other decorative shapes. Affix the cutouts to the top crust with the egg wash. Brush the top crust and any decorations with the egg wash.

Bake the pie until the crust is golden brown and the apples are tender when tested with a knife tip through the steam vent, 40–45 minutes. Let cool on a wire rack for 10 minutes, then serve warm with ice cream.

FOOD FOR THOUGHT

Florence White was England's first freelance food journalist, a remarkable accomplishment for a woman in the early twentieth century. In *Downton Abbey*, we witness the struggles Lady Edith endures while pursuing a career as a columnist. For centuries, women raised in great households were meant to be quiet and beautiful. But the times were changing, and Florence White was part of that change.

White founded the English Folk Cookery Association in 1928 and went on to publish a number of books on cookery and domestic subjects. Her best-known book, *Good Things in England*, appeared just four years after the founding of the association. A collection of more than eight hundred recipes sent to her by people from all over England, it was—and is—a valuable account of rural cooking in England dating back to the fourteenth century. In 1935, she published the *Good Food Register*, a directory of restaurants and other establishments that offered and celebrated English cooking.

All of White's work was focused on educating her readers on the importance of their English culinary heritage. In her later life, she returned to Fareham in Hampshire, where she had lived with her aunts as an eighteen-year-old and where she had first been introduced to traditional English cooking. There she established a cookery and domestic training school. Her last book, *Good English Food, Local and Regional*, was published posthumously in 1952.

CHRISTMAS CAKE

The term *Christmas cake* first appears in England in the nineteenth century. Before then, recipes for this type of cake in cookery books were simply titled "a good cake," "a good cake for Christmas," or just fruitcake or plum cake. These early cakes were never iced.

The first iced Christmas cake appears on the twelfth day of Christmas under the name Twelfth cake. Popular from the mid-eighteenth to the mid-nineteenth century, it was more bread-like than cake-like, was not as rich and dense as a fruitcake, was both iced and elaborately decorated, and had a "good luck" bean or, later, silver trinket baked in it. It was the English Epiphany cake, and it disappeared along with the custom of celebrating the Twelve Days of Christmas. The fruitcake adopted the icing typical of the Twelfth cake and became the Christmas cake, and the Christmas pudding took up the custom of the lucky trinket.

Ideally, you will make this cake well in advance of Christmas; the first day of Advent is a good beginning date. That's because this cake, like a plum pudding, gets better with time—and with regular additions of brandy or whisky.

SERVES 8–10

INGREDIENTS

¾ cup (170 g) unsalted butter, at room temperature

¾ cup (170 g) firmly packed dark brown sugar

3 tablespoons plus 2 teaspoons (60 g) golden syrup

2 eggs

1¼ cups (300 ml) whole milk

1 lb (450 g) dried currants

¼ lb (115 g) candied citrus peel, chopped

2 tablespoons blanched whole almonds, coarsely chopped

1 tablespoon skinned sweet apricot kernels, very finely chopped

1¾ cups (225 g) flour

Brandy or whisky, for drizzling

Preheat the oven to 275°F (135°C). Line the bottom and sides of a 7-inch (18-cm) springform pan with a double layer of parchment paper. Cut 2 squares of brown paper, such as mailing paper, a little larger than the pan and set aside. Cut a strip of brown paper the height of the pan and long enough to wrap completely around the outside of the pan.

In a bowl, using a wooden spoon, beat together the butter and sugar until light and creamy. Add the golden syrup and beat until blended. Add the eggs one at a time, beating after each addition. Now, gradually add the milk while stirring constantly. When all the milk is combined, fold in the currants, citrus peel, almonds, and apricot kernels. Finally, gradually fold in the flour until fully incorporated.

Spoon the batter into the prepared pan. Wrap the brown-paper strip around the outside of the pan and secure with kitchen string. Place a square of brown paper directly on the oven rack and set the pan on it. Place the second square on top of the cake. Bake the cake until a thin wooden skewer inserted into the center comes out clean, about 3 hours.

Let cool in the pan on a wire rack for about 1 hour, then unclasp the pan sides, transfer the cake to the rack, and let cool completely. Using the skewer, poke several holes in the top of the cake, then drizzle 3–4 teaspoons brandy evenly over the surface. Wrap the cake in parchment, store in an airtight tin in a cool cupboard, and repeat the addition of brandy once a week until Christmas. To serve, decorate the cake with fruit and nuts or white icing (see page 196).

A DOWNTON CHRISTMAS CAKE

In the kitchen of Downton Abbey, we see two Christmas cakes, one decorated with fruits and nuts and one covered in snow-white icing. The recipe on page 195, which comes from a 1920 cookery book, can be treated either way. You can also cloak your holiday cake in fondant (sugarpaste) for a more modern take (see opposite).

FRUITS AND NUTS

¼ cup (70 g) apricot jam

Selection of blanched almonds, walnuts, hazelnuts, and dried and candied fruits

In a small saucepan, warm the jam over medium heat until fluid, then pass through a fine-mesh sieve into a bowl. Using a pastry brush, brush the warm jam over the top of the cake. Arrange the nuts and fruits on top in an attractive pattern, pressing gently so they adhere to the glaze.

ROYAL ICING

About ½ cup (140 g) apricot jam

Confectioners' sugar, for dusting

About 1½ lb (680) marzipan

FOR THE ICING

3 egg whites

5½ cups (660 g) confectioners' sugar, sifted

1 tablespoon fresh lemon juce

Set the cake on a cake board or cutting board. In a small saucepan, warm the jam over medium heat until fluid, then pass through a fine-mesh sieve into a bowl. Using a pastry brush, brush the warm jam over the top and sides of the cake.

Lightly dust a work surface with sugar and place the marzipan on it. Knead until soft and pliable, then shape into a thick disk. Lightly dust a rolling pin and the disk with sugar and roll out the marizpan into a thin round large enough to cover the top and sides of the cake, checking as you work to make sure the marzipan isn't sticking to the surface. Roll the marzipan onto the pin, then gently unroll it over the cake. Using your palms, carefully smooth the marzipan over the top and sides until flat. Trim away the excess marzipan. Leave the cake to dry uncovered at room temperature for 2–3 days. (This prevents oil in the marzipan from seeping into the icing, marring it.)

To make the icing, in a large bowl, using an electric mixer, beat the egg whites on low speed until frothy. Add the sugar, a spoonful at a time, continuing to mix on low speed until all the sugar is incorporated and soft peaks form. Beat in the lemon juice. Increase the mixer speed to medium and beat until thick, stiff peaks form. This can take several minutes.

Using an icing spatula, spread the icing over the top and sides of the cake, making it as neat or as rustic as you like. Transfer the remaining icing to a piping bag fitted with your preferred decorating tip (or use multiple bags and different tips) and decorate the cake as desired. (Any leftover icing will keep refrigerated for up to 3 days.) Let the cake rest in a cool, dry place until the icing has set, at least 2 hours, then transfer to an airtight container until ready to serve.

SAVARIN

A close relative of the rum baba, the *gâteau Savarin* was invented by the Parisian pâtissier Auguste Julien in 1845 in honor of the great gastronome Jean Anthelme Brillat-Savarin. By the early twentieth century, the cake was popular in England, and John Kirkland gives several versions in his multivolume work, *The Modern Baker, Confectioner and Caterer*, published in London between 1907 and 1909. Kirkland says that babas and Savarins are a class of fermented cakes that are mostly of French origin and are sold in high-class confectioners' shops. People would buy them dry and then soak them in syrup at home.

Savarins, both large ones and individual ones, are baked in a ring-shaped pan. The cake is then unmolded and the center is typically filled with cream and different fruits, depending on the season. Kirkland includes photographs of Savarins decorated with cherries, apricots, and preserved fruits, one of them finished with sliced almonds and others left plain. While rum was traditional, *crème de noyaux* and maraschino or birch liqueur were also frequently used for flavoring the syrup

SERVES 8–10

INGREDIENTS

FOR THE SAVARIN

2 teaspoons active dry yeast

½ cup (120 ml) plus 1½ tablespoons tepid milk (105°–115°F/41°–46°C)

2¾ cups (345 g) bread flour

2 tablespoons superfine sugar

5 eggs

Grated zest of 1 lemon

1 cup (225 g) unsalted butter, melted and cooled

¾ cup (110 g) dried currants (optional)

⅓ cup (55 g) finely chopped candied citrus peel (optional)

FOR THE PAN

1 teaspoon rice flour

1 teaspoon confectioners' sugar

Unsalted butter, for greasing

FOR THE SYRUP

1½ cups (300 g) superfine sugar

6½ tablespoons (100 ml) water

Juice of 1 lemon

½ cup (120 ml) rum, kirsch, or maraschino or orange liqueur

FOR THE FILLING (OPTIONAL)

1¼ cups (300 ml) heavy cream

2 tablespoons confectioners' sugar

1 vanilla bean, split lengthwise

Sliced fresh fruit or berries of choice

To make the Savarin, in a bowl, dissolve the yeast in ⅓ cup (80 ml) of the tepid milk and and let stand until bubbly and foamy, about 5 minutes. Add ½ cup (60 g) of the flour and stir with a wooden spoon until a wet dough forms. This bubbly mixture of flour, liquid, and yeast is known as a sponge, and it yields a cake with a better, deeper flavor. Cover and let stand at room temperature for 1 hour.

In a large bowl, whisk together the remaining flour and the superfine sugar. Add the eggs one at a time, beating with a wooden spoon after each addition until blended. Add the lemon zest and stir well, then gradually add the butter and the remaining milk, beating until blended and a rough mass forms. Knead well in the bowl until the dough comes together, then add the risen sponge and continue to knead until a wet dough forms, about 10 minutes. The dough will be softer, stickier, and more flowing than the usual yeast dough. Sprinkle the currants and citrus peel on top, if using, then fold them into the dough, distributing them evenly.

To prepare the pan, in a small bowl, mix together the rice flour and confectioners' sugar. Butter a 23–24-inch (9–9½-inch) Savarin pan or Bundt pan, then dust with the flour-sugar mixture, tapping out the excess.

Transfer the dough to the prepared pan; it should be half full. Cover the pan with plastic wrap and let the dough rise in a warm spot until it is nearly to the rim, 30–60 minutes.

Meanwhile, make the syrup. In a saucepan, combine the superfine sugar, water, and lemon juice and bring to a simmer over medium heat, stirring to dissolve the sugar. Stir in the rum and simmer for a few minutes to evaporate some of the alcohol or longer to evaporate more of it. Remove from the heat and let cool.

Preheat the oven to 350°F (180°C).

Uncover the pan, place in the oven, and bake the cake until golden brown and a toothpick inserted into the center comes out clean, 20–25 minutes. Let cool in the pan on a wire rack for 5 minutes, then invert a second rack on top, invert the racks together, and lift off the rack and pan.

Pour half of the cooled syrup into the pan and carefully return the cake to the pan, immersing it partially in the syrup. Leave the cake to cool completely in the pan, where it will slowly soak up the syrup. When cool, pour the remaining syrup into a deep plate large enough to hold the cake and place the cake on the plate. Let sit for 30 minutes before serving.

While the cake is cooling, make the filling, if using. In a bowl, combine the cream and confectioners' sugar. Using the tip of a knife, scrape the seeds from the vanilla bean into the bowl. Using an electric mixer on medium-high speed or a whisk, whip the cream until soft peaks form. Cover and refrigerate until needed.

The cake can be served plain or with the whipped cream and fruit. If serving with the cream and fruit, spoon the cream into the center of the cake, or transfer the cream to a piping bag fitted with a large plain or decorative tip and pipe the cream into the center. Top the cream with the fruit and serve immediately.

MATTHEW: *You were wrong about one thing.*

MARY: *Only one? And what is that, pray?*

MATTHEW: *I never would . . . I never could, despise you.*

~ SEASON 2, EPISODE 9

HAZELNUT CAKE WITH COFFEE ICING

Published in 1925, *The Gentle Art of Cookery* devotes a number of pages to recipes that will intrigue the modern home baker, including this elegant buttercream-cloaked hazelnut cake. Its texture is delightfully spongy, and its nutty flavor is perfectly rounded off by the rich coffee-infused icing. Although the cake requires no decoration, roasted halved or whole hazelnuts would be a nice addition, especially if they are treated to a shiny caramel coating before they are placed on top.

SERVES 6–8

RECIPE NOTE

This buttercream recipe will yield more than you need for this small, rich cake. Any leftover buttercream will keep in an airtight container in the refrigerator for up to 5 days.

INGREDIENTS

Unsalted butter, for the pan

2 cups (220 g) hazelnut flour, plus more for the pan

¼ cup (10 g) fresh bread crumbs

½ teaspoon baking powder

2 eggs, separated

1 cup (200 g) granulated sugar

FOR THE BUTTERCREAM

1 cup plus 1 tablespoon (240 g) unsalted butter, at room temperature

3½ cups (400 g) confectioners' sugar

2 heaping teaspoons instant coffee dissolved in 1 tablespoon hot water, cooled

Preheat the oven to 350°F (180°C). Butter a 7-inch (18-cm) springform pan, then lightly dust with flour.

In a medium bowl, whisk together the flour, bread crumbs, and baking powder. In another medium bowl, using an electric mixer, beat the egg whites on medium-high speed until stiff peaks form. In a large bowl, using the electric mixer, beat together the egg yolks and granulated sugar on medium-high speed until pale yellow and fluffy. On low speed, add the flour mixture and beat just until blended. Using a rubber spatula, fold in about one-third of the beaten whites to lighten the mixture, then gently fold in the remaining whites just until no white streaks are visible.

Scoop the batter into the prepared pan and smooth the top with the spatula. Bake the cake until the top is golden brown and a toothpick inserted into the center comes out clean, 45–60 minutes. Let cool in the pan on a wire rack for 5 minutes, then remove the pan sides, slide the cake off the pan bottom onto the rack, and let cool completely.

To make the buttercream, in a bowl, using the electric mixer, beat the butter on medium speed until it is smooth and turns almost white. (This step is important to ensure a fluffy result.) On medium-low speed, add the confectioners' sugar, a spoonful at a time, and beat until it is completely absorbed. Finally, add the instant coffee and beat on medium-high speed until the buttercream is smooth and fluffy.

Transfer the cake to a serving plate. Using an icing spatula, cover the top and sides of the cake with the buttercream. If desired, spoon some buttercream into a piping bag fitted with a star or other decorating tip and pipe pretty borders onto the cake.

WARDLEY CAKE

Generously laced with stem ginger, this cake, which comes from Lady Agnes Jekyll's *Kitchen Essays*, turns out somewhat like a cake-size scone. Jekyll does not explain the source of the name, but many of the recipes in her book were given to her by friends, including perhaps an acquaintance from the town of Wardley, in north east England. The ginger and cherries make this cake a light alternative to the richer and darker Christmas Cake (page 195) without compromising on flavor.

SERVES 6–8

INGREDIENTS

I cup (225 g) unsalted butter, plus more for the pan

1¾ cups (225 g) all-purpose flour, plus more for the pan

½ lb (225 g) stem ginger in syrup

1½ cups (225 g) rice flour

I cup plus 2 tablespoons (225 g) superfine sugar

½ teaspoon baking powder

½ cup plus 1½ tablespoons (140 ml) whole milk

16 glacé cherries, quartered

Preheat the oven to 325°F (165°C). Butter the bottom and sides of a 9-inch (23-cm) round cake pan or an 8-inch (20-cm) square cake pan, then dust with all-purpose flour, tapping out the excess.

Drain the ginger, reserving the syrup. Chop the ginger into ¼–⅓-inch (6–8-mm) pieces. Set the ginger pieces and syrup aside separately.

In a large bowl, whisk together the all-purpose and rice flours, sugar, and baking powder. In a small saucepan, warm the milk over medium heat just to a simmer, then remove from the heat, add the butter, and let stand until the butter melts and the mixture is cool. Add the milk-butter mixture to the flour mixture and use a rubber spatula to bring the batter together, mixing well. Fold in the ginger and cherries, making sure they are evenly distributed throughout the batter.

Spoon the batter into the prepared pan, leveling the top with the spatula. Bake the cake until a toothpick inserted into the center comes out clean, 45–60 minutes. Let cool in the pan on a wire rack for 10 minutes, then invert the pan onto the rack, lift off the pan, and turn the cake upright. Brush the cake with the reserved ginger syrup. Or you can leave the cake plain, if you prefer. Let cool completely before serving.

GINGERBREAD BISCUITS

Gingerbread, which has a long history in much of Europe, first appeared in English cookery books in the late fourteenth century. It was often molded into human shapes—frequently lovers, sometimes even kings and queens—using a wooden mold. According to *The Oxford Companion to Sugar and Sweets*, Elizabeth I commanded her kitchen to shape gingerbread to resemble her courtiers, suitors, and others, which she would then have served to them. By the early nineteenth century, a similar custom was popular at local fairs, where gingerbread "husbands" were bought by girls looking for a sweetheart. Simpler shapes, such as large squares and freeform biscuits, were sold as well, both at fairs and at bakeries. In the Victorian era, gingerbread figures became popular Christmas-tree ornaments.

This recipe from Eliza Acton's 1845 book, *Modern Cookery*, was so popular that Florence White included it in *Good Things in England*, published in 1932. An old-style gingerbread, it calls for black treacle, which yields a pungent result. For a milder flavor, swap out the black treacle for golden syrup or light molasses.

MAKES ABOUT THIRTY-SIX 2-INCH (5-CM) BISCUITS

INGREDIENTS

1¾ cups (225 g) flour, plus more for the parchment and the mold (if using)

1 tablespoon ground ginger

¼ teaspoon ground allspice

¼ teaspoon ground mace

6 tablespoons (85 g) unsalted butter, at room temperature

¼ cup (60 g) firmly packed dark brown sugar

½ cup (170 g) black treacle or dark (medium) molasses

Preheat the oven to 275°F (135°C). Line 2 sheet pans with parchment paper.

In a large bowl, whisk together the flour, ginger, allspice, and mace. Add the butter and, using your fingers, rub it into the flour mixture until the mixture is the consistency of coarse bread crumbs. Add the sugar and stir with a wooden spoon until fully incorporated. Pour in the treacle and mix until blended. Now knead the dough in the bowl until smooth and evenly dark.

Lay a sheet of parchment paper on a work surface, dust it lightly with flour, place the dough in the center, and pat it into a thick, flat disk. If using a cookie cutter, roll out the dough a scant ¼ inch (6 mm) thick. Using a cutter in any shape you like, cut out as many biscuits as possible. Transfer them to the prepared pans, spacing them about ¾ inch (2 cm) apart. Gather up the scraps, roll out, cut out more biscuits, and add to the pans.

If using a wooden gingerbread mold, roll out the dough about ⅓ inch (8 mm) thick or thicker, depending on the depth of the carving. Dip the mold into water and dust lightly with flour. Cut a piece of rolled-out dough about 1¼ inches (3 cm) larger than the carving. Lay it on the prepared mold, then roll the rolling pin over the mold, pushing the dough into the carving. Trim any excess dough from the edge of the mold and turn the biscuit out onto a prepared pan. Repeat to make as many biscuits as possible, adding them to the pans and spacing them about 1 inch (2.5 cm) apart. Gather up the scraps, roll out, press out more biscuits, and add to the pans.

Bake the biscuits, rotating the pans back to front halfway through baking, until crisp, about 30 minutes. Let cool on the pans on wire racks for 5 minutes, then transfer the biscuits to the racks and let cool completely.

WHITBY YULE CAKE

In *Good Things in England,* Florence White notes this recipe is from a Lady Robinson, who submitted it for White's 1931 English Folk Cookery Exhibition. In the note that accompanied the entry, Lady Robinson explained that the recipe actually came from an elderly lady who served the cake along with a glass of cherry brandy to friends who visited her every year between Christmas and New Year's Day.

In the nineteenth and early twentieth centuries, being part of these visiting rituals was important to upper-class women, evidence of which we see in *Downton Abbey.* Hostesses for whom entertaining did not come naturally were under great pressure to serve the right refreshments and provide interesting conversation. That Lady Robinson's friend served the same cake to her friends each holiday season must mean they approved of it—or maybe they just endured it.

This cake is somewhat drier than other Christmas cakes, which makes a glass of brandy the perfect pairing, just as Madeira was traditionally poured to accompany Madeira cake.

SERVES 16

INGREDIENTS

¾ cup (170 g) cold unsalted butter, cut into cubes, plus room-temperature butter for the pan

2¾ cups (345 g) flour

½ cup plus 1 tablespoon (120 g) firmly packed dark brown sugar

1 tablespoon ground cinnamon

½ teaspoon ground nutmeg

1 egg

3½ tablespoons (50 ml) brandy

3½ tablespoons (50 ml) heavy cream

¾ cup (115 g) raisins

¾ cup (115 g) dried currants

Scant ½ cup (80 g) chopped candied citrus peel

⅔ cup (100 g) whole natural almonds

Preheat the oven to 275°F (135°C). Butter the bottom and sides of a 9-inch (23-cm) square baking pan. Line the bottom and two opposite sides of the pan with a strip of parchment paper, allowing the paper to overhang both sides by 1–2 inches (2.5–5 cm).

In a large bowl, whisk together the flour, sugar, cinnamon, and nutmeg. Scatter the butter over the flour mixture and, using your fingers, work the butter into the flour mixture until the mixture is the consistency of bread crumbs. Whisk together the egg and brandy, add to the flour mixture along with the cream, and stir and toss with a fork to moisten evenly. Add the raisins, currants, citrus peel, and almonds and, using your hands or 2 wooden spoons, mix together just until all the ingredients are evenly distributed and a rocky dough forms. Do not be tempted to add more liquid.

Press the dough into the prepared pan, leveling the surface with the palm of your hand. Using a sharp knife, score the dough into 16 squares, cutting halfway through the dough.

Bake the cake until almost rock-like to the touch, about 2 hours. Remove from the oven and, using the parchment overhang, lift it out of the pan onto a wire rack, pulling away the paper. Let the cake cool completely, then break or cut into the scored squares to serve. Store any leftover cake in an airtight container at room temperature for no more than 3 days, as it is quite dry already and will turn stale quickly.

DIY CHRISTMAS CRACKERS

It is impossible to imagine a Christmas feast in the United Kingdom without Christmas crackers. They are enjoyed by young and old, and if you make them yourself, you can tailor the treats inside to your guests. Sweets and a paper crown are traditional, but you can replace the small plastic trinkets found in many commercial crackers today with something special. A little strip of paper printed with a message is also a cracker staple. You can personalize the message to each guest, or you can create a game by turning the messages into questions that your guests have to answer.

The secret behind the magical "pop" the Christmas cracker makes when it is pulled apart is most commonly silver fulminate, a highly explosive silver salt of fulminic acid. It sounds pretty scary, and trying to make it at home isn't a good idea. Fortunately, you can buy cracker snaps or bonbon snaps in craft shops and online. These are narrow, two-layer strips of thin cardboard ready to install into your homemade cracker. The popping "explosive" is safely trapped between the layers, and when the cracker is pulled apart, the friction created by the motion creates the iconic pop.

YOU NEED
Wrapping paper, three cardboard toilet-paper tubes, scissors, double-sided tape or glue stick, cracker snap, ribbon, and candy, a small gift, a paper crown, and/or a message to put inside the cracker

METHOD
Line up the three toilet-paper tubes end to end on the center of a sheet of wrapping paper. The paper should be the length of the lined-up tubes and be wide enough to cover the tubes with a little overlap. Slip the cracker snap between the paper and tubes and secure it on both ends to the paper with a bit of tape or glue. Apply a line of double-sided tape or glue to an inside edge of the paper. Then roll up the tubes in the paper, covering them completely, and press the adhesive edge to seal. You now have a three-part tube covered in wrapping paper.

To create the cracker shape, pull out one of the outer tubes slightly and twist and turn the paper between the tubes. Tie the twist with a piece of ribbon to secure it in place, then pull out the outer tube from the end. Drop your chosen gifts into the opposite open end of the cracker, secure that end the same way, and remove the outer tube.

EXCELLENT TRIFLE

The recipe given here is for an early style of trifle, without any colorful layers of jelly or fruit. Instead, the trifle architecture consists of layers of boozy biscuits, custard, and syllabub, just as the first English trifles did in the 1750s. The result is excellent and complex, despite the absence of the later embellishments.

The syllabub layer is actually a dish on its own. In the eighteenth century, syllabub was regularly served at parties in special bell-top glasses, with each serving decorated with a rosemary sprig. There were three different types: Plain syllabub mixed together sweetened, spiced milk and cider or ale, which was left to curdle, producing a light froth on top and a boozy whey underneath. Whipped syllabub, which called for cream instead of milk and added more alcohol, created a creamier, more solid froth, which was eaten with a small spoon before the booze below was drunk. The everlasting syllabub called for cream and less alcohol, so it did not separate, making it suitable for trifles such as this one.

SERVES 8–10

INGREDIENTS

FOR THE CUSTARD

1¼ cups (300 ml) whole milk

1¼ cups (300 ml) heavy cream

3 tablespoons Demerara sugar

1 blade mace

1 fresh bay leaf

6 egg yolks

FOR THE SYLLABUB

½ cup (120 ml) white wine, such as sweet Riesling

⅓ cup (80 ml) fresh lemon juice

¼ cup (60 ml) sherry or Madeira

1¾ cups (425 ml) heavy cream

½ cup (50 g) confectioners' sugar

7 oz (200 g) lady fingers (sponge fingers)

7 oz (200 g) ratafia biscuits or amaretti

6½ tablespoons (100 ml) sherry or Madeira

3½ tablespoons (50 ml) brandy

Seasonal greenery, for decorating

First, make the custard. In a saucepan, combine the milk, cream, Demerara sugar, mace, and bay leaf and bring to a gentle simmer over medium heat. Remove from the heat and let infuse for a few minutes. Meanwhile, in a bowl, whisk the egg yolks until blended.

Remove the mace and bay from the milk mixture and bring back to a simmer. Remove from the heat and slowly add about ½ cup (120 ml) of the hot milk mixture to the egg yolks while whisking vigorously. This tempers the yolks so they will not cook when the remaining hot milk mixture is added. Then slowly add the remaining hot milk mixture, bit by bit, whisking until smooth. Pour the contents of the bowl into the saucepan, place over low heat, and cook, stirring constantly with a wooden spoon, until the mixture is smooth, slightly thickened, and coats the back of the spoon, about 5 minutes. Remove from the heat and pour through a fine-mesh sieve into a pitcher. Cover with plastic wrap, pressing it directly against the surface of the custard to prevent a skin from forming, and let cool completely.

To make the syllabub, in a small bowl, stir together the white wine, lemon juice, and sherry. In a medium bowl, whisk together the cream and confectioners' sugar until the sugar dissolves. Add the lemon juice mixture and whisk constantly until the cream thickens to soft peaks. (You may want to use an electric mixer for this step, as making syllabub by hand can take 10–15 minutes of steady whisking.)

Recipe continues

To assemble the trifle, select a footed clear glass bowl 7½–8 inches (19–20 cm) in diameter. Arrange half of the lady fingers and ratafia biscuits in a single layer on the bottom of the bowl. Drizzle half of the sherry and then half of the brandy evenly over the top. Arrange the remaining lady fingers and ratafias in a single layer in a second bowl and drizzle them with the remaining sherry and brandy. Pour the cooled custard evenly over the lady fingers and ratafias in the glass bowl. Transfer the liquor-soaked lady fingers and ratafias from the second bowl to the glass bowl, arranging them on the custard. Spoon the syllabub on top. Cover and refrigerate for at least 1 hour or up to 4 hours.

To serve, if using a footed bowl, decorate the foot with greenery. If using a regular bowl, set it on a large, attractive plate and decorate the plate rim with greenery. Scoop the trifle directly from the bowl to serve.

MARY: *You must say it properly. I won't answer unless you kneel down and everything.*

He does.

MATTHEW: *Lady Mary Crawley, will you do me the honour of becoming my wife?*

MARY: *Yes!*

~ SEASON 2, EPISODE 9

TUTTI-FRUTTI ICE CREAM

Tutti-frutti, colored chunks of candied fruits, has been combined with ice cream in England since the 1860s, either mixed into the ice cream itself, dotted on top, or both. Nowadays, the term often refers to Indian candied papaya, but in the Victorian era, English cooks would have more commonly turned to candied citrus, cherries, and angelica. Look for the Indian product, typically labeled "tutti-frutti mix," in South Asian grocery stores and online.

SERVES 4–6

RECIPE NOTE

Do not skip the step of mixing the candied fruits with the sherry and liqueurs a day in advance of making the ice cream, as it ensures the fruits won't dry out during freezing.

INGREDIENTS

½ lb (225 g) candied fruits, finely chopped, or store-bought tutti-frutti

1 teaspoon maraschino liqueur

1 teaspoon sherry

1 teaspoon curaçao

2½ cups (600 ml) heavy cream

½ cup plus 1 tablespoon (110 g) sugar

4 egg yolks

The day before you plan to make the ice cream, combine the candied fruits, maraschino liqueur, sherry, and curaçao in a bowl and leave to soak at room temperature overnight. Drain the fruits, reserving the fruits and alcohol separately.

Put a 9 x 5 x 3-inch (23 x 13 x 7.5-cm) loaf pan into the freezer to get ice-cold.

In a saucepan, combine the cream, sugar, and reserved alcohol and bring to a simmer over medium heat, stirring to dissolve the sugar. Remove from the heat and pour into a heatproof pitcher. In a bowl, whisk the egg yolks until blended. Slowly drizzle the warm cream mixture into the egg yolks while whisking constantly to create a smooth custard. Let cool completely.

Pour the cooled custard into the ice-cold loaf pan and return the pan to the freezer for 45 minutes. Remove the pan from the freezer and, using a rubber spatula, thoroughly stir the custard, bringing any frozen edges into the center. Return the pan to the freezer for 30 minutes.

After 30 minutes, stir the custard thoroughly as before, again making sure you scrape any of the frozen custard from the edges into the center. Return the pan to the freezer. Continue to repeat this step of freezing the custard for 30 minutes, stirring it, and then returning the pan to the freezer for 30 minutes. The mixture will get thicker and thicker at the edges of the pan each time you leave it in the freezer for 30 minutes until finally you have ice cream. This will take 2–3 hours.

When your ice cream is the perfect consistency, set aside 2 tablespoons of the candied fruits for garnish and fold the remaining fruits into the ice cream. Return the pan to the freezer for 30 minutes. Scoop the ice cream into dessert glasses, dot with the reserved candied fruits, and serve.

NESSELRODE ICE PUDDING

Chestnuts and candied fruits have long been traditional flavors at Christmastime in Britain. This chestnut-laced ice cream pudding, which was created by famed French chef Antonin Carême in honor of a Russian count and diplomat, appeared in many English cookery books throughout the nineteenth century. It was often made in a dome-shaped mold and decorated with a sprig of holly to mimic a boiled Christmas pudding. Disguising food in this manner had been a popular English custom since medieval times, an illlustration of how the British upper class enjoyed a bit of humor—and theater—at the dinner table.

SERVES 4–6

INGREDIENTS

2½ tablespoons dried currants

2 tablespoons glacé cherries

1 tablespoon chopped candied lemon and/or orange peel

1 tablespoon dark rum

1 tablespoon maraschino liqueur

2½ cups (600 ml) heavy cream

¼ cup (50 g) firmly packed dark brown sugar

1 bay leaf

Grated zest of 1 lemon

4 egg yolks

5 jarred or vacuum-packed roasted and peeled whole chestnuts

The day before you plan to make the pudding, combine the currants, cherries, citrus peel, rum, and maraschino liqueur in a small bowl and leave to soak at room temperature overnight. This step will prevent the fruits from drying out during freezing.

Put a 9 x 5 x 3-inch (23 x 13 x 7.5-cm) loaf pan into the freezer to get ice-cold.

In a saucepan, combine the cream, sugar, bay leaf, and lemon zest and bring to a simmer over medium heat, stirring to dissolve the sugar. Remove from the heat and pour through a fine-mesh sieve into a heatproof pitcher. In a bowl, whisk the eggs yolks until blended. Slowly drizzle the warm cream mixture into the egg yolks while whisking constantly to create a smooth custard. Let cool completely.

Meanwhile, using a mortar and pestle, grind the chestnuts to a fine powder.

Pour the cooled custard into the ice-cold loaf pan and return the pan to the freezer for 45 minutes. Remove the pan from the freezer and, using a rubber spatula, thoroughly stir the custard, bringing any frozen edges into the center. Return the pan to the freezer for 30 minutes.

After 30 minutes, stir the custard thoroughly as before, again making sure you scrape any of the frozen custard from the edges into the center. Return the pan to the freezer. Continue to repeat this step of freezing the custard for 30 minutes, stirring it, and then returning the pan to the freezer for 30 minutes. The mixture

Recipe continues

will get thicker and thicker at the edges of the pan each time you leave it in the freezer for 30 minutes until finally you have ice cream. This will take 2–3 hours.

When your ice cream is the perfect consistency, fold in the ground chestnuts and the soaked fruits and their soaking liquid and transfer it to a decorative 2½-cup (600-ml) mold or a freezer-safe airtight container. Cover and place in the freezer for the final freezing, at least 2 hours or up to overnight.

To serve, if you have used a mold, fill a bowl with hot tap water. Dip the bottom half of the mold into the water for 10 seconds, then invert the mold onto a serving plate, tap the bottom of the mold with your hand, and lift off the mold. This might take a few tries. Cut into wedges with a knife, dipping it into hot water before each cut, and serve on small plates. If you have not used a mold, scoop out with a spoon, dipping the spoon into hot water before each scoop, and serve in dessert glasses.

Edith turns to Marigold.

Well, we're together darling. And I know it's not ideal, but it's such an improvement on being apart, that I think we should celebrate. I'll order ice cream and a glass of Champagne and we'll be as jolly as you like.

She smiles at Marigold and rocks her in her arms.

~ SEASON 5, EPISODE 6

RIPON SPICE BREAD

In *Good Things in England*, a collection of recipes from the English countryside, Florence White includes this bread, which she credits to Mr. Herbert M. Bower, who describes it as a "cake" for serving on Christmas and New Year's Eve. Adding generous measures of raisins and currants to holiday baked goods seems to have been common in the historic Yorkshire town of Ripon, as this quote from a 1790 issue of *The Gentleman's Magazine* suggests: "At Rippon [*sic*], in Yorkshire, on Christmas Eve, the Grocers send each of their customers a pound, or half a pound of currants and raisins to make a Christmas Pudding."

White's original recipe instructs the reader to use bread dough and to add the rest of the ingredients to it. There are no directions for making the dough, as bread dough was often made in big quantities in large households and then used to make different style breads. Commercial bakers would also make a plain dough and then make a variety of buns from it. This spice bread is reminiscent of the old-style cakes that were made with yeast instead of baking powder and is similar to the Welsh tea bread known as bara brith.

SERVES 6–8

INGREDIENTS

4 cups (500 g) bread flour, plus more for the work surface

1 cup plus 2 tablespoons (220 g) sugar

1 tablespoon active dry yeast

1 teaspoon ground allspice

1¾ teaspoons sea salt

1⅓ cups (325 ml) water

1 cup (225 g) lard or unsalted butter, melted and cooled

1½ cups (220 g) raisins

1½ cups (220 g) dried currants

⅓ cup (60 g) finely chopped candied citrus peel

In a large bowl, whisk together the flour, sugar, yeast, allspice, and salt. Make a well in the center and pour half of the water into the well. Using a wooden spoon, draw the flour into the well until a dough begins to form, gradually adding the remaining water as you work. Then gradually add the lard, continuing to mix until a rough mass forms. The dough will be rather wet, but don't be alarmed. Using your hands, knead the dough in the bowl until it is uniform, soft, and fairly smooth, about 10 minutes. Add the raisins, currants, and citrus peel and fold in until evenly distributed. Cover the bowl with a damp kitchen towel and let the dough rise in a warm spot until doubled in size, about 1 hour.

Line the bottom of a 9 x 5 x 3-inch (23 x 13 x 7.5-cm) loaf pan with parchment paper. Punch down the dough and turn out onto a floured work surface. Flatten the dough into a thick disk, then, starting at the edge closest to you, roll up the dough and pinch the seam together. Fold in both ends toward the seam, pinching to seal in place. You should have a fat sausage shape. Place the dough, seam side down, in the pan. Cover the pan with the damp towel and let the dough rise in a warm spot until doubled in size, about 1 hour.

Toward the end of the rising time, position a rack in the lower third of the oven and preheat to 425°F (220°C).

Bake the bread until the top is golden brown, about 35 minutes. To test if the bread is ready, turn the loaf out of the pan and tap the bottom with a firm thump. If it sounds hollow, it's ready. Let cool completely on a wire rack before serving.

CHAMPAGNE JELLY

No Downton dinner would be complete without some form of molded jelly or cream, and the one featured here is one of the simplest and the most elegant. It was served at Edward VII's coronation banquet in 1902, and it is a lovely addition to a Christmastime table. Champagne itself appears regularly at Downton, most obviously on occasions such as New Year's and at the numerous weddings.

SERVES 6

IVY: *Well, what do you want?*

JIMMY: *To have a good time. To see the world. To meet beautiful women and spend money and drink Champagne.*

IVY: *You can't make a career out of that.*

JIMMY: *Some people do. I want a life that's fun.*

~ **SEASON 4, EPISODE 4**

INGREDIENTS
---

1 bottle (750 ml) Champagne or other sparkling wine

2 envelopes (2½ teaspoons each) powdered gelatin, or 8 gelatin sheets

2 tablespoons water, if using powdered gelatin

½ cup plus 1 tablespoon (115 g) sugar

Berries and/or edible flowers (optional)

Fresh mint leaves, for garnish

Put the Champagne bottle into the freezer 30 minutes before you start the recipe. This step ensures the bubbles will stay in the final jelly. In a small bowl, sprinkle the powdered gelatin over the water and let stand until softened, 3–5 minutes. If using gelatin sheets, put the sheets into a bowl, add cold water to cover, and let soak until floppy, 5–10 minutes.

Open the Champagne and pour ½ cup (120 ml) into a small saucepan. Return the Champagne to the freezer if you can stand the bottle upright. If not, put the bottle into the refrigerator. Add the sugar to the saucepan, place over medium heat, and heat, stirring, until the sugar dissolves. Remove from the heat. Liquefy the powdered gelatin by setting the small bowl of softened gelatin into a larger bowl of very hot tap water. If using gelatin sheets, lift the sheets from the water, wring gently to release excess water, and then put them into a small bowl and liquefy as for powdered gelatin. Add the liquefied gelatin to the Champagne mixture and stir until the gelatin dissolves. Strain the mixture through a fine-mesh sieve into a bowl or pitcher and let cool to room temperature.

Add 2 cups (480 ml) of the chilled Champagne to the cooled gelatin mixture and stir well. If adding embellishments to the gelatin, pour half of the gelatin mixture into a 2½-cup (600-ml) mold and refrigerate until almost set, 30–45 minutes; arrange the embellishments on top, then add the remaining gelatin mixture. If serving the jelly without embellishments, pour all the gelatin mixture into the mold. Cover the filled mold and refrigerate until fully set, at least 8 hours or up to 1 day. (If the time of day is right, you can sip the remaining Champagne.)

To serve, fill a bowl with hot water. Dip the bottom of the mold into the hot water for a few seconds to loosen the jelly from the mold, then unmold the jelly onto a serving plate. Garnish with mint.

EPIPHANY TART

Dorothy Hartley, who chronicled the food in England in her well-known book of the same name, was born in Yorkshire in 1893. She trained as a teacher and began teaching in 1920, but was soon writing and traveling extensively on the side. Five years later, she published, along with coauthor Margaret Elliot, her first book, volume one of the six-volume *Life and Work of the People of England*. Although *Food in England* was not published until 1954, she lived and traveled during the period in which Downton is set and observed the lives of people all over Britain in that time.

In *Food in England*, Hartley mentions this striking star tart made with a dozen different jams and includes an illustration, but she provides no recipe for it, explaining only that it was made for church socials on Epiphany. Don't feel as if you must create such an intricate design. A simple cross and four types of jam—or the six-pointed star and three types of jam—will still be impressive.

SERVES 8–10

INGREDIENTS

FOR THE SHORTCRUST PASTRY

2 cups (250 g) flour, plus more for the work surface

¾ cup plus 2 tablespoons (100 g) confectioners' sugar

Pinch of sea salt

½ cup plus 1 tablespoon (125 g) cold unsalted butter, cut into cubes

1 tablespoon water

1 egg yolk

1 egg yolk beaten with 1 tablespoon whole milk, for egg wash

3 to 12 different jams in a variety of colors

To make the shortcrust pastry, in a bowl, whisk together the flour, sugar, and salt. Scatter the butter over the flour mixture and, using your fingers, rub the butter into the flour mixture until the mixture resembles bread crumbs. In a small bowl, whisk together the water and egg yolk. Add the yolk mixture to the flour mixture and mix with your hands until the flour mixture is evenly moistened and the dough comes together in clumps.

Turn the dough out onto a lightly floured work surface and knead gently and briefly until it comes together in a single mass. Wrap in plastic wrap and refrigerate for 30 minutes.

Preheat the oven to 400°F (200°C). Have ready an oven-safe 10-inch (25-cm) enameled-metal dinner plate.

Unwrap the dough, return it to a lightly floured work surface, and knead briefly until smooth. Place a large square sheet of parchment paper on the work surface and set the dough on the center of the parchment. Pat the dough into a thick disk, then, using a rolling pin, roll out the dough into a round ⅛ inch (3 mm) thick. Place the enameled dinner plate, bottom side up, on the dough round. With a small knife, cut around the edge of the plate. Clear away all the excess pastry from around the plate and set it aside for making the star.

Slide your hand under the parchment and lift and flip the plate over right side up. Peel off the parchment and gently press the pastry against the bottom and sides of the plate. Prick the pastry all over with a fork. Set the pastry-lined plate to one side.

Recipe continues

Clean the work surface and lightly dust again with flour. Gather together the pastry scraps, place on the floured surface, and gently knead them together. Pat into a thick rectangle and then roll out into a rectangle ¼ inch (6 mm) thick and at least 10 inches (25 cm) long. Cut the rectangle lengthwise into strips ⅔ inch (1.5 cm) wide and 9½ inches (24 cm) long. Trim any ragged ends. Using 3 strips, create the first triangle on the pastry-lined plate. Make sure the points extend to the rim of the plate, as later you will be laying a pastry ribbon on top of the rim to hide the outer edges where the points are crimped to the rim.

When you are satisfied with the shape of your triangle, carefully brush a little of the egg wash underneath the strips, then position them back into the tidy triangle. Now use your thumb and index finger to squeeze the strips together ever so slightly to create dam-like walls to contain the jam. Crimp the ends of the pastry strips onto the rim, leaving the pointy tips tidy. Now create a second triangle on the plate the same way, positioning it to create a six-sided star. Use your fingers to squeeze the pastry rim so it becomes thinner. If the rim is thicker than the rest of the pastry, it won't cook as quickly.

Knead the remaining pastry back together into a narrow bar and then roll it out into a long strip ¹⁄₁₆ inch (2 mm) thick and the width of the rim of the plate. The strip needs to be about 32 inches (82 cm) long to cover the rim completely. If you are anxious about attempting to use a single strip, make 2 or 3 strips or as many as you are comfortable with handling. It is important that you cover the spots where you squeezed the points of the star into the rim. Brush the pastry rim with the egg wash, then place the strip(s) on top, pressing gently to secure in place, and trim the edges with a sharp knife.

Carefully spoon the jams into the openings of the star, playing with the colors to create something that looks like a stained-glass window. Try not to get jam on the pastry. If you do, use the back of a spoon to tidy up your work.

Use a fork or other tool to decorate the rim and further crimp the strip to the pastry. Brush all the visible pastry with the egg wash. Bake the tart until the pastry is golden brown, 20–25 minutes. Let cool completely on a wire rack before serving.

FOOD FOR THOUGHT

Elaborate tart designs were common in England in the seventeenth and eighteenth centuries, and famed chef and author Robert May includes many illustrated examples of them in *The Accomplisht Cook*, which he published in 1660, the year of the Restoration. While Dorothy Hartley describes these tarts in a country setting of church socials in the 1920s, the tarts of the seventeenth and eighteenth centuries were found on the tables of the upper class.

YULE-DOUGH

According to John Brand in *Observations on Popular Antiquities of Great Britain*, published in 1777, the yule-dough was a small cake in the shape of the baby Jesus that bakers made at Christmastime to give to their customers. Also known as a yule-dow (the words *dough* and *dow* were once commonly used for small cakes in northern England) and, in County Durham, as a yule-cake, these yeast-leavened sweets were more bread-like than cake-like.

Ben Jonson referred to these sweets in his Jacobean-era "Christmas, His Masque," a holiday entertainment that played at court in 1616. The lead character is a personified Christmas, who is accompanied by "sons and daughters," among whom are not only Mumming (folk plays) and Post and Pair (a popular card game of gamblers) but also Mince-Pie and Baby-Cake, evidence that all of these were established traditions in the era.

Recipes for yule-doughs from that time are unknown, which means they are very much the food of the common people, baked in a bakery but not at court. Cakes like these can still be found in some localities today.

MAKES 4 SMALL CAKES

INGREDIENTS

---

8 cups (1 kg) bread flour, plus more for the work surface

⅔ cup (125 g) superfine sugar

1¾ teaspoons sea salt

1 teaspoon active dry yeast

5 tablespoons (70 g) unsalted butter, cut into small cubes, at room temperature

2 eggs, lightly beaten

2½ cups (600 ml) tepid whole milk (105°–115°F/41°–46°C)

1 egg yolk, lightly beaten, for egg wash

Unsalted butter or jam, for serving

In a large bowl, whisk together the flour, sugar, salt, and yeast. Make a well in the center and scatter the butter in the well. Pour the eggs and half of the milk over the butter and, using a wooden spoon or rubber spatula, draw the flour into the well and mix until evenly combined. Gradually add the remaining milk, stirring until fully combined and a shaggy dough forms. The dough will be rather wet, but don't be alarmed. Knead in the bowl until you get a soft, wet dough, about 10 minutes. Then cover the bowl with plastic wrap and leave the dough to rest at room temperature overnight (or a maximum of about 8 hours).

The next day, preheat the oven to 400°F (200°C). Line a sheet pan with parchment paper.

Turn out the dough onto a lightly floured work surface and divide it into quarters. Shape each quarter into a small figure of a baby. This can be a very simple shape, using one-fourth of the dough for the head and the rest shaped into an oval for the body. You can then take it a step further and use a wet knife to cut through the dough on either side of the oval for two little arms and then cut the bottom of the oval about two-thirds of the way up for the legs. The shape of the figure will wither a bit during baking, so just an indication that it is a figure is sufficient. Transfer the figure to the prepared pan and repeat with the remaining dough quarters, spacing them evenly apart.

Brush the figures generously with the egg wash. Bake until golden brown, 15–20 minutes. Let cool on the pan on a wire rack for at least a few minutes before serving. Then serve warm or at room temperature with butter.

ANNA

Mr. Carson likes to serve two white wines, which you should open and decant just before they eat. A light one for the hors d'oevres. Then a heavier one with the soup. Keep that going for the fish and then change to Claret, which you should really decant now. There's a pudding wine and, after that, whatever they want in the drawing room with their coffee.

MOLESLEY

Blimey. It's a wonder they make it up the stairs.

~ SEASON 2, EPISODE 8

DRINKS

MULLED WINE

The earliest known spiced, or mulled, wine appeared in a first-century Roman cookery book, and similar spiced wines were drunk in the Middle Ages, though they were usually served cold not warm. Recipes for hot mulled wine and beer do not begin to show up until the eighteenth century, and then they typically contain egg yolks, which results in a thick, rich drink. By the Victorian era, mulled wine no longer included eggs.

In *Modern Cookery*, published in 1845, Eliza Acton gives a recipe for mulled wine, noting that sherry or ginger wine can replace the port, in which case four egg yolks are a good addition—a throwback to the eighteenth-century custom. The recipe here is adapted from Acton's, with two primary changes: orange juice replaces water for simmering the spices and a bottle of wine is used instead of a pint. You can also add a couple of egg yolks, whisking them until thick and creamy and then tempering them with a little hot wine before adding them to the pan. At Downton, mulled wine might be served to welcome the Christmas hunting party back from the forest, though the Crawleys would probably want their drink egg-free.

SERVES 4

INGREDIENTS

1 orange

6 tablespoons (80 g) sugar

1 teaspoon ground cinnamon

1 teaspoon ground ginger

24 whole cloves

1 bottle (750 ml) full-bodied red wine or port

Using a small, sharp knife, remove the peel from the orange in strips, then halve and juice the orange. Transfer the orange peel and juice to a saucepan large enough to accommodate all the wine and add the sugar, cinnamon, ginger, cloves, and ¼ cup (60 ml) of the wine. Place over medium heat and bring to a simmer, stirring to dissolve the sugar. Simmer until the mixture is reduced by half, about 5 minutes. (At this point, you can let the mixture cool, then cover and refrigerate for a few days until you are ready to finish and serve the wine.)

Add the remaining wine to the spiced syrup and heat over medium-low heat just until hot. Do not allow it to boil or you will burn off the alcohol. Remove from the heat and strain through a fine-mesh sieve into a heatproof punch bowl. Serve warm.

RECIPE NOTE

This mulled wine is very spicy. If you are accustomed to contemporary mulled wine, cut the amounts of ginger and cloves in half. You can then decide if you want to increase the amount of spices the next time you make the recipe.

ON ENGLISH PUNCHES

Cocktails make an appearance at Downton after World War I, when a mixed drink before dinner was becoming fashionable in Britain. The Dowager Countess is set against them because they are an American import, but she remains in favor of traditional English punches, which graced English Christmases and other festive occasions for the century before the entrance of the cocktail. These alcoholic winter warmers would have been familiar to all the Crawleys, from the sisters Sybil, Edith, and Mary to the Dowager Countess.

In *Cakes & Ale*, a collection of essays and recipes on food and drink published in 1897, author Edward Spencer writes that the word *punch* is generally believed to come from the Hindi word *panch*, or "five," for the five ingredients that go into every punch: spirit, acid, spice, sugar, and water. He does say that many punch recipes call for more than five ingredients and that some omit water, and then goes on to offer a large selection of punch recipes, warning first that it is absolutely necessary to use the "very best materials" for punch: "There must be no inferior sherry, Gladstone cleat, cheap champagne, nor potato-brandy, used for any of my recipes, or I will not be responsible for the flavour of the beverage."

Spencer's description of punch opens his chapter titled Compound Drinks and is followed by a varied array of punch recipes, among them a couple of milk punches, a Glasgow punch, an ale punch, and an Oxford punch. It closes with a recipe for a John Collins—soda water, lemon slice, curaçao, and gin—a forerunner of the early twentieth-century cocktail craze.

CAMBRIDGE MILK PUNCH

Milk punch is closely related to the medieval English posset, a warm drink of milk, wine or ale, and spices, and to eggnog, a cold drink of milk, cream, sugar, eggs, and brandy or other spirit. This recipe is taken from Eliza Acton's *Modern Cookery*, and given the name of the punch, this version was likely popular at the university. But milk punch was widely served throughout England, with Oxford, Norfolk, and other locales boasting their own versions. It is ideal for sipping after a day in the countryside, whether out hunting as the Crawleys did or out walking as is more common today.

SERVES 8–12

INGREDIENTS

I lemon

2 quarts (2 l) plus I cup (240 ml) whole milk

I cup plus 2 tablespoons (225 g) sugar

2 egg yolks

2½ cups (600 ml) light or dark rum

1¼ cups (300 ml) brandy

Using a small, sharp knife, remove the peel from the lemon in strips (reserve the remainder of the lemon for another use). In a large, heavy saucepan, combine 2 quarts (2 l) of the milk, the lemon peel, and sugar and bring to a simmer over medium heat, stirring to dissolve the sugar. While the milk is heating, in a bowl, whisk together the egg yolks and the remaining I cup (240 ml) milk until blended, then pour through a fine-mesh sieve into a pitcher.

When the sugar is fully dissolved and the milk is at a simmer, scoop out and discard the lemon peel. Slowly pour the egg yolk mixture into the simmering milk while whisking constantly. Then add the rum and brandy and continue to whisk vigorously until a light froth forms on top and the punch is piping hot. Pour into a heatproof punch bowl and serve right away.

Mrs. Hughes offers him one of the two glasses of punch she is carrying. Carson closes the door.

CARSON: *I don't think I should.*

MRS. HUGHES: *Go on. It's Christmas. Let's toast your new house.*

~ SEASON 5, EPISODE 9

ON WASSAIL

Wassail is a hot mulled punch usually made with cider, though a version made with ale, known as lambswool, is also popular. Recipes vary from county to county and orchard to orchard and have been part of the Christmas lore of the British Isles for centuries. The 1835 edition of *Oxford Night Caps*, a collection of drink recipes by Richard Cook, includes a recipe for lambswool that begins with these lines from seventeenth-century lyric poet Robert Herrick's *Twelfth Night, or King and Queen*:

> *Next crowne the bowle full*
> *With gentle Lambs wooll,*
>
> *Adde sugar, nutmeg, and ginger,*
> *With store of ale too,*
> *And thus ye must doe*
>
> *To make the Wassaile a swinger.*

The word *wassail* comes from the Old English term *was hál*, which was linked to the popular Anglo-Saxon salutation *wes þú hál*, loosely "be healthy." These early terms also spawned the word *wassailing*, the custom of singing and merrymaking in rural areas, usually apple-growing counties, on Twelfth Night. These festive outings included ceremonial drinking to the health of the apple trees to ensure a good harvest in the coming year, as these four lines from *Hesperides*, Robert Herrick's 1648 poetry collection, illustrate:

> *Wassail the trees, that they may bear*
> *You many a plum and many a pear:*
> *For more or less fruits they will bring,*
> *As you do give them wassailing.*

There is also a material culture connected to wassailing. Communal wassail bowls were made of pottery or turned wood, often with three or more handles for shared drinking. Later, in more upper-class circles, glass punch bowls and cups became the fashion and imbibing from a single bowl gradually disappeared from every level of society.

WASSAIL

Wassail, a hot mulled punch usually made with cider and sometimes with ale, has been part of British Christmastime festivities for hundreds of years. In the eighteenth century, it was the custom to invite friends and neighbors to play cards and to enjoy dinner together on Twelfth Night. The wassail bowl, full of roasted apples in sweet spiced cider or ale, was brought in at the end of the evening. First, each person scooped out an apple and ate it, and then the bowl was passed around the room and everyone would drink from it and wish one another good health.

By the era of *Downton Abbey*, the practice of drinking wassail had moved to Christmas and the roasted apples served only as flavoring and decoration. In season 5, episode 9, we see the kitchen table fully laden with the Christmas food preparations. Daisy is carefully preparing the turkey, and the footmen are in charge of transferring the wassail from copper kettles dotted with apples to glass punch bowls. Later, after singing carols by the Christmas tree, everyone helps themselves, ladling wassail into their glass cups.

SERVES 12–20

INGREDIENTS

2½ cups (600 ml) apple cider

¾ cup plus 2 tablespoons (200 ml) sherry

2 cups (450 g) firmly packed dark brown sugar

¼ teaspoon ground nutmeg

¼ teaspoon ground ginger

1 cinnamon stick

FOR SERVING

3 or 4 small apples

3 quarts (3 l) apple cider

2 lemons, thinly sliced

Shards of cinnamon bark (optional)

Preheat the oven to 350°F (180°C).

Combine the cider and sherry in a small saucepan over medium heat and bring to a simmer, making sure the mixture does not boil. Add the sugar, nutmeg, ginger, and cinnamon and simmer, stirring, until the sugar dissolves. Remove from the heat and let cool.

For serving, using a vegetable peeler, remove a strip of skin from around the equator of each apple. This allows steam to escape and prevents the apples from bursting in the oven. Arrange the apples in a small baking pan and roast until tender when pierced with a knife, 20–30 minutes. Let the apples cool.

When ready to serve, pour the spiced cider mixture and the plain cider into a large punch bowl and stir to mix. Pop the apples, lemon slices, and the cinnamon shards (if using) into the bowl for decoration. Ladle into cups and serve.

RECIPE NOTE

This wassail is served at room temperature, but if you prefer a warm punch, the spiced cider and the plain cider can be heated before they are added to the punch bowl.

SMOKING BISHOP

A popular Christmastime drink in Victorian England, this mulled punch famously appears near the end of Charles Dickens's *A Christmas Carol*. Scrooge, who has been given a second chance at life, surprises Bob Cratchit with a stream of kind words and the offer of "a Christmas bowl of smoking bishop."

In the 1827 *Oxford Night Caps*, a slim volume of recipes for alcoholic beverages "used in the university," the bishop is described as "[seeming] to be one of the oldest winter beverages known." Although most recipes feature lemon, bitter orange is sometimes used and may have been favored in older bishops, as this early eighteenth-century verse by Jonathan Swift suggests: "Come buy my fine oranges, sauce for your veal, / And charming, when squeezed in a pot of brown ale; / Well roasted, with sugar and wine in a cup, / They'll make a sweet bishop when gentlefolks sup."

As bitter oranges are unavailable in England until January or Feburary, lemon would have been used for the Christmas bishops at Downton. The recipe here is adapted from one in the 1913 edition of Edward Spencer's *Cakes & Ale*.

SERVES 4

INGREDIENTS

I lemon or bitter orange	I½ teaspoons ground allspice
6 whole cloves	I¼ cups (300 ml) water
FOR THE SPICE MIXTURE	I bottle (750 ml) red port
I½ teaspoons whole cloves	¼ cup (50 g) sugar
I½ teaspoons ground mace	Grated zest and juice of
I½ teaspoons ground ginger	½ lemon
I½ teaspoons ground cinnamon	Cinnamon sticks, for garnish (optional)

Score the peel of the lemon all over with a sharp knife and press the cloves into the peel, spacing them evenly around the fruit. Pierce the lemon onto a roasting fork. Using the gas flame on a stove top or a kitchen torch, roast the peel of the lemon on all sides. Be careful not to blacken the skin.

To prepare the spice mixture, in a small saucepan, combine the cloves, mace, ginger, cinnamon, allspice, and water and bring to a boil over medium heat. Boil until reduced by half, 8–10 minutes. Meanwhile, in a medium saucepan, combine the port, sugar, and lemon zest and juice and bring to a simmer over medium heat, stirring to dissolve the sugar.

When the spice mixture is ready, pour it into the port mixture, stir well, and heat until piping hot. Do not allow the mixture to boil. Remove from the heat and pour through a fine-mesh sieve into a heatproof punch bowl. Pop the roasted lemon into the bowl and garnish with cinnamon sticks, if desired. Serve warm.

FOOD FOR THOUGHT

According to historian Elizabeth Gabay, the bishop, port laced with spices, belongs to a group of warm spiced drinks called "ecclesiastics," which also includes the pope, made with Champagne or Burgundy, and the cardinal, made with claret or Rhine wine (though sources differ on these pairings, with some linking the pope with Tokay and the cardinal with Champagne). The addition of the word *smoking* to all these wintertime warmers was meant to evoke the steam rising from the punch bowl in which they were served.

EGG-FLIP

The egg-flip, which is similar to American eggnog but without the milk or cream, is related to the posset, a dairy-based alcoholic concoction that dates back to medieval times and remained popular for centuries among the English upper class. The term *flip* comes from the recipe direction to pour, or "flip," the finished drink between two jugs for a couple of minutes just before serving "to froth the flip thoroughly." Of egg-flip and its kin, ale-flip (which includes butter in addition to eggs), Edward Spencer, author of *Cakes & Ale*, says, "more-ish on a cold evening; and no Christmas Eve is complete without a jug of one or the other."

Lady Grantham, who grew up in America, would have known—and likely preferred—eggnog over egg-flip. But she may have found it difficult to convince Mrs. Patmore to prepare something new and would have had to settle for the near-identical egg-flip. In contrast, her mother, Martha Levinson, would have certainly preferred the richer American version with bountiful amounts of rum and brandy and would not have hesitated to make that clear.

SERVES 4

INGREDIENTS

2½ cups (600 ml) ale

6 tablespoons (80 g) sugar

I egg

Freshly grated nutmeg, for garnish

Ground ginger, for garnish

In a saucepan, combine the ale and sugar and bring to a gentle simmer over medium heat, stirring to dissolve the sugar. Remove the pan from the heat. In a small bowl, whisk the egg until frothy, then gradually add the egg to the ale while whisking constantly.

You need 2 pitchers (the ideal) or 2 deep bowls. Pour the mixture into a pitcher or bowl, then pour the mixture back and forth between the 2 pitchers or the 2 bowls until it is frothy. (You can opt for the more modern method of whisking the mixture vigorously until frothy.)

Pour or ladle into glasses or cups and top each serving with a light grating of nutmeg and a tiny pinch of ginger. Serve warm.

FOOD FOR THOUGHT

In the seventeenth and eighteenth centuries, upper-class men carried a nutmeg grater made of silver or other precious metal in their vest pocket for topping their cup of punch with the freshly grated spice.

ROBERT: *I want everybody to have a drink!*

~ SEASON 5, EPISODE 9

ACKNOWLEDGMENTS

I dedicate this book to my friend and mentor Dr. Annie Gray, food historian and author of several fascinating books. I know no one who simultaneously loves and loathes Christmas with such great—and equal—passion as she does. She firmly and stubbornly dislikes the modern Christmas we often think of as traditional but adores with great zestfulness the real English Christmas of plum pudding served with roast beef, meaty mince pies, and boar's head on the side. Thank you for everything over the years and, in this book, for your reflections on Christmas (page 10).

Thank you to Amy Marr and Roger Shaw at Weldon Owen and to the people at Carnival for believing in me to create this book. It was written during the 2020 pandemic lockdown, which provided great challenges not only for sourcing ingredients to test recipes but also for organizing such integral parts of the book as the design, editing, and photography, the latter finally able to happen in New York City the week the lockdown was eased. Each person who had a role in this process has had a difficult job because of the pandemic, which makes this book a triumph not only for me but for everyone involved. Thank you all very much.

I also wish to thank Dom, Tessa, and Jan at Northfield Farm, who answered all my butchery questions remotely when travel was prohibited during the lockdown; famed English pottery company Mason Cash for sending a pudding bowl for the photo shoot with such speed during a time of postal disruptions; Netherton Foundry in Shropshire for generously helping with a pie pan; and the many people on Twitter who advised me on game when there was no game to be had in the market.

Finally, a word of thanks to my parents, who helped eat all the festive food, and to my beloved husband, who always loses me when I dive into research and never seem to come up for air. Merry Downton Christmas to you all.

ABOUT THE AUTHOR

Born in Flanders, Belgium, Regula Ysewijn is a noted authority on British culinary history. Among her books are *Pride and Pudding: The History of British Puddings Savoury and Sweet* and *Oats in the North, Wheat from the South* (published in the United States as *The British Baking Book*), which tells the story of how the diverse climate of the British Isles influenced the cultivation of cereal crops and the development of a rich regional baking identity. She is the resident culinary historian and judge on the Flemish version of the television series *The Great British Bake Off* and has consulted and presented for British television and radio productions. She has also written for various British and international institutions and publications and contributed to *The Official Downton Abbey Afternoon Tea Cookbook*. At the age of eight, Regula began teaching herself English by reading Jane Austen and watching historical documentaries and costume dramas on the BBC, the one British television channel that was available in Belgium. This started a lifelong passion for British culture and social history, with a particular interest in food.

INDEX

weldon**owen**

CEO Raoul Goff
Publisher Roger Shaw
Associate Publisher Amy Marr
Creative Director Chrissy Kwasnik
Designer Debbie Berne
Photo Shoot Art Director Marisa Kwek
Production Manager Binh Au
Editorial Assistant Jourdan Plautz

Photographer John Kernick
Food Stylist Cyd Raftus McDowell
Prop Stylist Suzie Myers

Produced by Weldon Owen
1150 Brickyard Cove Road
Richmond, CA 94801
www.weldonowen.com

Library of Congress Cataloging-in-Publication
data is available.

ISBN-13: 978-1-68188-535-3

Printed in the United States of America
First printed in 2020
10 9 8 7 6 5 4 3 2 1

Weldon Owen wishes to thank the following
people for their generous support in producing
this book: Rizwan Alvi, Annie Gray, Charlotte
Havelange, Rae Hellard, Don Hill, David Ludtke,
Eve Lynch, Elizabeth Parson, and Sharon Silva.

Weldon Owen also wishes to thank:
Julian Fellowes; Gareth Neame, Margaret Parvin,
Charlotte Fay, and Nion Hazell at Carnival
Films; Daisy Chandley and Annabel Merullo
at Peters Fraser and Dunlop; Benoit Adam,
Cindy Chang, Kristin Conte, and Megan Startz
at NBCUniversal; and Laura Martlew at the
Portmeirion Group.

Photos on page 113 (Yorkshire Christmas
Pie) and page 116 (Boar's Head Terrine)
by Regula Ysewijn

Recipes on page 45 (Palestine Soup), page 165
(Oysters au Gratin), and page 216 (Champagne
Jelly) reprinted from *The Downton Abbey Cookbook*
by Annie Gray

Cover image: Plates by Spode. For traditional
English china, please visit www.spode.com